THE
FIRST "REAL" JOB

SUNY Series, The New Inequalities
A. Gary Dworkin, Editor

THE
FIRST "REAL" JOB

A Study of Young Workers

Kathryn M. Borman

STATE UNIVERSITY OF NEW YORK PRESS

Published by

State University of New York Press, Albany

© 1991 State University of New York

For information, address State University of New York
Press, State University Plaza, Albany, N.Y., 12246

Production by E. Moore
Marketing by Bernadette LaManna

Library of Congress Cataloging-in-Publication Data

Borman, Kathryn M.
    The first "real" job : a study of young workers / Kathryn M.
Borman.
        p. cm. — (SUNY series, the new inequalities)
    Includes bibliographical references (p.   ) and index.
    ISBN 0–7914–0598–2 (Ch. : acid-free) . —ISBN 0–7914–0599–0 (Pb. :
acid-free)
    1. Youth—Employment—United States—Case studies. 2. Industrial
sociology—United States—Case studies. I. Title. II. Series:
SUNY series in the new inequalities.
HD6276.U62B67   1991
331.3′4′0973—dc20   90-9910
                                                                   CIP

10 9 8 7 6 5 4 3 2 1

This book is dedicated with love to Walter C. Borman III, Ph.D., who has often helped me to see the big picture and the smallest details in it.

CONTENTS

PREFACE

In 1942, as wartime labor production accelerated, a book titled *Barriers to Youth Employment* was published by the American Youth Commission, a group established by the American Council of Education to promote policies addressing the needs of youth. Inadequate educational preparation for work, lack of access to particular jobs, and youths' competition with adults for jobs were major barriers to the full employment of young people seeking work. These problems have a familiar ring in the early 1990s, a situation suggesting that this society has perennial difficulties in accommodating young people in the transition from school to work.

The social and economic context has changed considerably in the last fifty years, but the relationship of young people to the labor market is still problematic. Although difficulties remain for these youths, the focus recently has not been on their needs and concerns. The educational reform reports, including such volumes as *A Nation at Risk* and *The Good High School*, have ignored issues confronting the large percentage of high school seniors who do not complete four years of college. What kind of curriculum and teaching during high school are most helpful to the 75 percent of high school seniors who either do not enter or do not complete college but instead become workers? How can teachers, employers, and the young workers themselves become empowered to understand the marketplace of youth jobs? These questions have not been addressed or answered in the educational reform literature. This book provides an understanding of the school-to-work transition to assist researchers, students, and others in comprehending the workplace demands typically encountered by young workers and in understanding their responses to those demands.

The analysis does not stop here, however. The case studies of young workers profiled in this book describe systematically and in detail the process of becoming established as a young worker in our society. The research reported here generated more than fifty thousand pages of observational notes, interview data, and related materials. A team of five social scientists followed twenty-five young workers into forty-six work sites, including an appliance repair shop, a factory that produces industrial staples, a sheet metal shop, several banks and insurance companies, a coin and stamp store, and a health spa. These sites were the locales for these young workers' first "real" jobs in the sense that the youths held these positions for at least six months and viewed them as means of entrée to adult responsibilities. The investigators also talked with the young people, their employers, their parents, and their friends and acquaintances in their homes, in their cars, at restaurants, at work, and in courts of law. The goal was not only to learn about adolescent workers and work, but also to place their work experiences in the context of their daily lives. Team members were well aware of the complaints that youths are indifferent to work, have little concern for their own career development, and make irresponsible, poorly trained, and badly motivated workers (Snedeker 1981). By following youths through their daily routines at work and off the job we hoped to come to understand these young people's experiences as fully as possible and to confirm, modify, or amend the negative view of adolescent workers that exists in our society.

This book is an important resource for youths, their parents, their teachers, and their employers as well as for those who consider and formulate policy governing youths and work. The goal in writing this book is to contextualize these young workers' experiences in the youth labor market, in the developmental issues facing all adolescents, and in work and educational policy. In an important sense, this book is really about a critical period in the life course, the transition from school to work, for a group who left high school in the early 1980s.

This cohort as a whole has confronted and will continue to confront reduced economic opportunities in comparison to older and younger groups in society. In 1983 and 1984 they told us about how "there ain't no jobs," a condition that does not prevail in our relatively affluent times. Thus work and the significance of work are likely to have a rather different meaning for the twenty-five adolescents who participated in this study and for their peers born in the early 1960s than for their younger brothers and sisters, for whom less (in population numbers) is more (in economic and related opportunities). As adolescents coming of age in an era of relatively scarce job opportunities, these young people are less sanguine about their job prospects and about prospects for happy lives in general.

Lest this study seem to be a gloomy testament to a lost generation, we wish to underscore the point that we found these youths to be remarkably resilient, vibrantly optimistic, and eagerly self-confident. Adolescence, after all, is the time of expansiveness and high energy (Csikszentmihalyi and Larson 1984). Unlike their far more cautious elders, most young people share a sense of delight in life even while they are vulnerable and at risk because of labor market conditions and structural constraints.

There are scores of labor market profiles of youth, authored chiefly by economists, but those studies consider aggregate data on cohorts of young workers rather than individual cases (e.g., Freeman and Wise 1982; Osterman 1980). They include surveys of the effects of employment policies and programs on youths' subsequent workplace successes and failures. Most of these studies, however, conclude that difficulties in seeking and finding work are rooted in the family and social structure and therefore are beyond the grasp of traditional labor market approaches. This analysis is an attempt to move beyond these earlier studies by looking at work in the full fabric of contemporary adolescents' lives. These case studies illustrate the issues that youths confront, the persistence of underemployment, and the distance between the presentation of skills in schools and the experience of jobs in the workplace.

This book addresses a number of questions about the lives of young workers in a variety of work settings. The settings selected for investigation correspond with the three major labor market sectors employing young workers in the United States: manufacturing, banking and insurance, and the new service economy businesses. Research sites corresponding to the manufacturing sector included a factory and a large welding shop, industrial settings that fifty years ago typified workplaces employing youths, particularly male workers. Two large financial corporations and one insurance firm represented businesses in the "old" service economy, which also traditionally hired young workers in the past. In the traditional service sector, low-level clerical jobs are held primarily by young women in financial, insurance, and real estate businesses. Finally, since the 1950s a third kind of setting has developed as a major employer of young workers. These workplaces frequently demand that employees regulate feelings and subvert the norms of social exchange in the interest of selling a service. Hochschild (1983) has referred to this form of labor as "emotion work." Sites representing "new" service industries in this study included a health spa, where "emotion work" often combines with physical skill and talent in young workers' jobs, and a coin and stamp store, perhaps the most democratic and the richest learning environment we entered during the research.

In conducting this research, we took the case study approach. The case study has long been an important conceptual and methodological tool for researchers focused on the social system of the workplace (Holtzberg and Giovanni 1981; Simpson, 1989). Holtzberg and Giovanni (1981) state the following in their review of case study research conducted in the 40s and 50s:

> The industrial firm was a popular setting in which to carry out research because it offered an optimum context for the study of the dynamics of social interaction and group structure. It also lent itself to objective "scientific" investigation with the help of rigorous methodologies that could obtain measurable, quantifiable, verifiable and generalizable data (327).

Most case studies in industrial settings carried out in the 1940s and 1950s used experimental or quasi-experimental research designs and focused on the "scientific" description of human relations, considering such issues as leadership patterns and qualities, the hierarchical ordering of authority, cliques and friendship groups, factors affecting the shop climate, the adjustment of women, ethnics, and members of racial minorities in a particular plant setting, and—not surprisingly, in view of the concern with quantification—the productive efficiency of line employees (Holtzberg and Giovanni 1981). The research generated by the case method in those years was preoccupied with the industrial setting as a "primitive isolate," a community unto itself. The implications of most of these studies were policy-related and were targeted at improving workers' efficiency and productivity. In addition, the research, influenced by the code of efficiency, was keyed to the technology of a goods-producing manufacturing economy.

In many of the settings investigated in this book, however, material goods are not the final outcome of workers' efforts. In fact, most of the workplaces employing young workers nationally and in the study are service-producing enterprises. According to the National Bureau of Labor Statistics, services in the U.S. economy reference everything *not* related to the production of durable goods. The goods-producing sector includes farming, mining, construction, and manufacturing. Job performance in these businesses is gauged by how many products (beans, rice, coal, buildings, widgets) are grown, extracted, or fabricated, and how efficiently. In contrast, high productivity in jobs in the service sector is difficult to measure. It is not only difficult but also probably "unscientific" to attempt to evaluate the quality of the emotion work carried out by a receptionist at a health spa or a dancer at a major amusement park.

A major purpose of this study is to clarify how a young worker's location in the labor market is reflected in patterns of social relationships rather than in simple "output" in the workplace. The methodology involved the use of the comparative case study approach. The research team was present in a cross-section of service- and goods-producing industries. The questions addressed were generalizable across these work domains. Our intent was that research outcomes would provide richly descriptive data to suggest policies and practices that would allow schools to become more effective in preparing youths for work. I have not used material from all twenty-five cases here simply because the ten or so cases described in the book contain the most detailed and most complete information. The greatest amount of information, not surprisingly, emerged for participants in the study who stayed in the same job for at least nine months. We were fortunate that so many young workers remained employed in the same jobs for this length of time; the average time on the job for young workers is six months.

The initial framework for this study was based on the following set of questions:

• How does work experience vary according to the workplace habitus or job setting in which the young employee works?
• Do young women have different work experiences from young men? To what extent do other individual characteristics, such as race, social class, and cultural capital, mediate job experience?
• How do work tasks vary across settings? How, especially, do tasks in goods-producing jobs differ from tasks in service jobs?
• How do social relationships on the job and outside the context of work affect work experience?

The findings documented in this book will provide at least preliminary answers to these questions.

ACKNOWLEDGMENTS

As I attempt to give proper acknowledgment to all those who encouraged me in undertaking a study of youth at work and completing the task of writing this record of that research, I am aware that there have been many who have made this enterprise possible.

First, I owe considerable thanks to Ellen Greenberger, whose advice to the National Institute of Education (NIE) prompted the funding of this study in 1983. Ron Bucknam, project monitor at NIE, was always supportive of this study, and I am grateful for his assistance. John Bishop, the project director for this study, and Dick Miquel at the National Center for Research in Vocational Education (NCRVE) at Ohio State had the vision to see that large-scale studies of youth labor-market behavior should be supplemented by close observational work in case studies, and in particular by the studies reported in this volume. The research could never have been carried out without the sometimes herculean efforts of Jane Reisman, my co-principal investigator and good friend to whom I am especially grateful, and to our team of field workers: Lisa Chiteje, Margo Vreeburg Izzo, Renee Keels, Shirley Piazza, and Beth Penn. Once the data were "in the can," we received considerable support from NCRVE staff in putting up countless pages of field notes, organizing and coding passages with empirically-derived descriptors, and getting fancy software to yield good old ethnographic data with an up-to-date technological twist. To all who participated in this process and especially to Margo Izzo, who supervised and shepherded the study through this phase, I owe considerable thanks.

I am indebted to Philip Wexler, who saw the value in pulling a book-length manuscript together and to Wally Borman, to whom this book is dedicated and who gave well-informed and loving attention to various chapter drafts. I also wish to thank Jeylan Mortimer, Gary Fine, William T. Pink, Margaret LeCompte, Richard Lakes, and Rhoda Halperin, all of whom provided helpful comments on various drafts of the book. Gary Dworkin, who edited the series in which this volume appears, Lois Patton, Floyd Hammack, and two anonymous reviewers at SUNY Press, and Elizabeth Moore, Production Editor at SUNY Press, helped the volume through a final set of revisions. Karen Feinberg's editorial work substantially improved the volume, while Dale Wilburn and Ruth Pedersen took the manuscript through a number of revisions with great skill and patience. Janet Duricy and Pat Timm labored to match references with material cited in the text. My enormous thanks to all.

Finally, of course, the largest debt is owed to the twenty-five young people in Columbus and Cincinnati who allowed us to examine their lives, particularly their lives at work, so closely. Their involvement in their work *and* in this study was inspiring. All were very eager to have their experiences at work and in related areas of their lives shared with others. I came away from the offices, factories, and other workplaces where the research was carried out with a strengthened belief in the altruism and essential goodness of youth. Last, but not least, thanks to my sons, Greg and Geoff, who were adolescents during the time of this research and writing and who frequently allowed me to test my theories of youth with them.

CINCINNATI, OHIO
AUGUST, 1990

1. CULTURAL REPRODUCTION THEORIES AND THE RELATIONSHIP BETWEEN SCHOOL AND WORK

IN 1985, 48 PERCENT OF graduating high school seniors in the United States did not go on to college the following fall or to any other formal, institutionally based training program (U.S. Department of Education 1986). In addition, not all who entered college remained there. Current patterns suggest that by their junior year, approximately 13 percent of students who begin college will have forsaken higher education; only 25 percent of those who entered as freshmen will complete their senior year four years later (U.S. Department of Education 1986).

In a nation that emphasizes the importance of education beyond high school, it may be difficult to comprehend data illustrating persistent, widespread patterns of movement to work from high school or before completion of college. Such immediate movement into a work setting with limited opportunities for a good salary or advancement in the firm seems especially incomprehensible because family financial difficulties, as indicated by the absence of a parent or by the heavy demands on family resources created by a large number of children, do not by themselves constrain enrollment in higher education (Borus and Carpenter 1984). The important point here is that three-quarters of those in a given cohort of high school graduates have not completed college four years after graduation; for the most part they have found jobs in the regular labor force.

This book examines the alternative routes to their occupational futures taken by those who leave school for work. Most members of this group enter the workplace to assume jobs in the service sector of the labor market, a point we will examine fully in chapter 2. This chapter is concerned with theoretical and research perspectives on the relationship between school and work in American society, particularly as it affects individuals during an important phase of the life course—the transition from school to work.

Over the years researchers, policymakers, and others have taken a variety of theoretical positions to understand the impact of work on the lives of young workers and the relationship of work to other social institutions, particularly school. The most recent theory that attempts to explain the transition from school to work was influenced heavily by Paul Willis and other so-called reproduction theorists, who argued that schools, as sorting mechanisms, perpetuate social, racial, and gender inequalities (Griffin 1985; Valli 1986; Willis 1977). According to reproduction theorists, successive generations of manual laborers are "reproduced" in school classrooms and on the shop floors of workplaces through their experiences as subordinates in a capitalist system that both denigrates manual (as opposed to mental) labor and keeps particular groups (women, African-Americans, and the working class) marginalized and cut off from access to the most desirable, best paying, least dirty work. While I believe that much can be learned from the cultural reproduction perspective, particularly from its concern with the marginalization of women and of racial, ethnic, and other social groups, a major problem with the theory is that it fails to take into account current labor market conditions governing workplace social relations and occupational trajectories.

The cultural reproduction theories to be reviewed in this chapter attempt to explain how the family, the school, the workplace, and other major societal institutions mold social relations in a capitalist economy. These theories hold (1) that social characteristics, including values, attitudes, and beliefs, are transmitted from one generation to the next; (2) that major social institutions, especially the family, the school, and the workplace, are the sites for social reproduction; and (3) that the "products" of social reproduction are members of a society deeply divided from one another in their access to material and nonmaterial rewards, relative power, and authority. Cultural reproduction theorists analyze the often hidden factors that shape decisions to remain in school or to leave school to seek employment. They argue that social relationships in these theories are not only fabricated, much like steel or like cars on an assembly line; they are also perpetuated and reproduced in the next generation. This aspect of social reproduction theory, despite the archaic quality of the central metaphor in the current era of service-sector growth, is perhaps the most compelling argument put forward by these theorists.

In chapters 3 through 5 we will see how a group of young workers in their first real jobs experienced, in factories, banks, insurance companies, and retail stores, social relationships that for the most part appeared to limit their opportunities dramatically. Among the twenty-five youths in this study who left high school in 1983 to enter the workplace rather than to attend college, the great majority were working-class children of working-class parents. By moving directly into the workplace, these individuals were at least in some form perpetuating or reproducing the social order "inherited" from their parents. Moreover, the best-paying jobs (in manufacturing) went to the young white male workers in this study; while the worst-paying positions with little or no opportunity for advancement, went to young women, particularly African-Americans.

Unfortunately, the metaphor for cultural reproduction is based on a manufacturing model of the economy, which emphasizes production of goods. This metaphor is ironic in a period when jobs in the service sector, which emphasize human relations and emotion work, are ascendant and when industrial jobs in the goods-producing sector are disappearing in the U.S. economy (Stanback and Noyelle 1982). We could view this model as a manifestation of a "Marxist hangover," because cultural reproduction theories are indebted most deeply to Karl Marx, who developed his political ideology when industrialism was on the rise in Western capitalist economies.

With respect to the labor market, cultural reproduction theories assume, first, that differentially valued sets of skills are required in different types of jobs in the labor market; second, that manual labor skills are denigrated most and rewarded least with material benefits and social prestige; and third, that verbal skills in social relations, mentoring, and persuading are highly prized, are rewarded handsomely, and are required only in jobs held by high-level managers.

As we will see, the reward system, job responsibilities, and opportunities for interaction with others and for initiative on the job have been altered dramatically by the new service economy. Thus cultural reproduction theory is flawed because of its lack of attention to current conditions governing the workplace, particularly in the new service economy jobs. For young workers in today's labor market, "bust ass" jobs in manufacturing are rewarded most highly by material benefits, while jobs in the service sector requiring human relations skills are far more demanding and financially less well-paying. Among the twenty-five young workers who participated in the study, the best-paid employee, a white male, worked as a material handler in a large factory that produced industrial staples. He earned almost $10 per hour in 1984, while the study was under way. The least well-paid workers were African-American and white women who held a variety of jobs, including gas station attendant, bank clerk, and food service worker, all of which paid the minimum wage. In addition, these young women were far more vulnerable than the other youth workers to the pressures that workers experience in performing jobs charged with "emotion work," a characteristic of occupations in the service sector. Hochschild's (1983) study of Delta Airlines workers reveals the high cost of "emotion work" to flight attendants, who constantly must mask their own affective responses to cater to demanding and frequently uncivil male passengers.

Of the three assumptions on which reproduction theories are built, at least two seem flawed. Recall that these theories support the claims that different jobs require different skills, that manual labor skills are least valued and least well paid, and conversely, that verbal skills are most highly valued and most handsomely paid. Although it is true that differentially valued skills are inherent in different forms of work across labor market sectors, it appears that manual skills command the greatest material rewards in today's youth labor market, though perhaps they are accorded lower social prestige. This point is open to empirical investigation. In contrast, the verbal skills required in retail and consumer-oriented enterprises are often accompanied by degraded emotion work and are rewarded by payment of the minimum wage.

Cultural reproduction theories explaining the relationship between school and work vary in the extent to which they emphasize economic determinism over individual action in molding outcomes. These outcomes range from the worker's personality characteristics and values to his or her labor market location in adulthood. The strongly deterministic models emphasize demands in society for a differentiated work force. In this variation of the cultural reproduction perspective, jobs are arrayed in pyramidal style paralleling the socioeconomic structure of society. The relatively scarce, prestigious positions in the highly rewarded professions are allocated to an elite corps drawn from the most economically favored groups, who possess the appropriate cultural capital and skills. (Cultural capital is the set of skills, such as knowledge of the computer, and of tastes, such as valuing gourmet cuisine, that families impart and that other institutions, such as the school, reinforce for particular groups.) In contrast, more individualistic theories emphasize the role of individual agency, emotions, temperament, and experiences in determining occupational outcomes. Theories in the middle range argue that culture, which is rooted in individual action, values, ideology, and material conditions, is reflected in social relations, which broadly influence individual outcomes.

In the next sections of this chapter I will analyze four strands of cultural reproduction theory: the determinist, the cultural capital, the subcultural, and the individual perspectives. My critique of the individual perspective concludes with a feminist analysis of the prevailing images that have dominated this frequently sexist theoretical position. Notwithstanding the contributions to our understanding of the connections among family, school, and work, I argue that cultural reproduction theories are not only subverted by an anachronistic emphasis on the production line as the modal work station in society; they are also weakened by a failure to critique the thinly veiled sexism that dominates the individual perspective in particular. Finally, in concluding the discussion of the relationship between school and work, I examine the encounters of youth with school-based and community-based school-to-work programs.

THE DETERMINIST PERSPECTIVE

In sociology of education, the determinist position has been articulated by researchers and theorists in structural analyses of the process of status allocation. This process refers to the influence of parental socioeconomic status (usually measured by father's occupation) on the child's (usually the son's) educational and occupational outcomes. The status attainment or status allocation process as it affects individuals over time is the most frequently examined process in contemporary American sociology. Factors influencing the process early in the life course include individual attitudes, skills, and personality as well as major institutional factors, particularly the family's material and nonmaterial resources and the school's organizational and structural arrangements. These arrangements include curricular tracking, which sorts students into academic, vocational, or general-studies "tracks."

One can argue that the most influential early study of social mobility was the work of Blau and Duncan (1967), which established the variables and measures that came to dominate this kind of research. In this and later studies, results suggested that although education and association with peers in school and in the neighborhood play a role in the status allocation process, the most important and most lasting influence is the family's position in the socioeconomic structure, presumably because of the access to education, cultural capital, and social skills that families may or may not provide. Current scholars in this camp hold a considerable range of positions. I will examine four: the economic, the gatekeeping, the tournament, and the cooling-out models.

The Economic Model

The most strongly determinist position of the four is represented in the work of Bowles and Gintis (1974), whose economic theory of social reproduction in school is intertwined graphically with an image of the industrial workplace in capitalist society. Specifically, Bowles and Gintis point to five parallel dimensions under current capitalist arrangements that strongly influence individual outcomes: (1) structural constraints governing relationships in schools and at workplaces, particularly in power and authority roles, (2) extrinsic systems of rewards and incentives (grades and wages), (3) lack of control over the contents of the curriculum and the contents of work tasks, (4) the competitive nature of work in school and at jobs, and (5) subject matter specialization in school and task fragmentation on the job. According to Bowles and Gintis's analysis, an almost perfect symmetry exists between socialization at school and accommodation to work.

One of the criticisms leveled at Bowles and Gintis is that their work is not based on strong empirical evidence. For example, Valli (1986), in her study of the schooling of future female clerical workers, demonstrates that much more individual choice in curricular programs governs course selection than Bowles and Gintis's position allows. Another criticism is that this formulation, like the traditional functionalist analyses challenged by Bowles and Gintis, is static; it does not allow for the dynamics of technological change in either the academic or the work sphere. Rather, in this strongly determinist view, economic laws of supply and demand govern a world of schooling and working dominated by the image of a goods-producing, assembly-line technology. Because most jobs in the U.S.

economy today are not in manufacturing, this conception is anachronistic. Less ironclad determinists have examined more closely the actual workings of the status attainment process in schools and have speculated about the parallels to a wider range of workplaces than those prevailing in the fading American industrial goods-producing economy. These theorists offer three alternatives to a rigidly deterministic correspondence model: the gatekeeping model, the tournament model, and the cooling-out model (Valli 1986).

The Gatekeeping Model

Among the three alternative models, the gatekeeping model explains most accurately the system of curricular placement that exists in virtually all American secondary schools. Curricular placement or tracking is the process by which students are sorted into one of two or three options: (1) the academic or college preparation track, which includes advanced mathematics and science courses and "accelerated" English and social studies coursework; (2) vocational studies, the "applied" course that includes a focus on one of several general areas such as clerical and retail work, construction and the manual trades, or child care and other "pinkcollar" skills; and (3) a general studies track, which provides students with a smattering of coursework across a wide range of academic and nonacademic studies, preparing them poorly either for higher education or for work after high school.

Variations in curricular placement by socioeconomic status and race or ethnicity have been documented widely. For example, in an extensive examination of secondary school tracking systems, Oakes noted that "poor and minority students are most likely to be placed at the lowest levels of the schools' sorting system" (Oakes 1985, 67). Moreover, rather than providing these groups with the increasing access to opportunities inherent in the academic track, the national system appears to be providing increasingly less opportunity. In their comparison of trends in enrollment in the three curricular tracks from 1972 to 1982, Eckstrom, Goertz, and Rock (1989) report the following:

> In 1972 more than two-thirds of high SES [socio-economic status] students were in the academic track but only about one-quarter of low SES students were in this curriculum. By 1982, both high and low SES groups had fewer students in the aca-

demic curriculum but high SES students were *four times* as likely to be in this curriculum track as low SES students (58).

School-based gatekeepers, particularly teachers and guidance counselors, often use inappropriate information, such as a student's suspension record, to inform track placement decisions, particularly whether a student is enrolled in an academic, a vocational, or a general course of studies. Students whose attendance rates are likely to be poorest are those with the most demands on their time outside school. Such students come overwhelmingly from economically disadvantaged families and are likely to be Hispanic, African-American, and white inhabitants of the central city attending the weakest schools (Wehlage and Lipman, 1988). Most student dropouts and unemployed young job-seekers are enrolled in general studies while in high school. In Cincinnati, which has a fairly typical central-city school system, 1987 failure rates were highest for students in the general track: 30 to 35 percent of all enrolled students failed classes as compared to 15 to 23 percent of students enrolled in academic-track classes. Further, the average general-track student took 5-1/2 years to complete 4 years of high school because of retention in grade.

According to the gatekeeping analysis of tracking, high school guidance personnel are preeminently important in the process of placing students as mentioned previously. Their primary source of information about students is the informal lore of the school, particularly teachers' opinions. Students' interests, their "objectively" assessed performance on tests, and their parental background fade in importance by comparison to their reputation, according to Cicourel and Kitsuse (1963) and others who hold to the gatekeeping model of curricular track placement. Empirical support for the gatekeeping model in explaining racial differences in track placement was offered recently by Eckstrom (1985) in her analysis of 1982 national High School and Beyond Survey data. Eckstrom determined from students' responses to a series of questionnaire items that 52 percent of African-American high school students reported being *assigned* to a track, whereas 58 percent of her white respondents had *chosen* their track.

The Tournament Model

The tournament model has been offered to explain how curricular track placement is contested ground, in which students vie for scarce positions at the top of the tracking system in secondary school. In addition, once students are placed in a curricular track, regardless of their prior performance on achievement tests, their classroom performance and their test scores begin to mirror the expectations governing outcomes for that particular track (Oakes 1985; Rosenbaum 1976). For instance, students who may have performed well in the past frequently suffer a decline in achievement as a result of placement in a low-achieving track. As we have seen, track placement can be capricious, based on a distorted analysis of students' most recent attendance records rather than on skills or interests. Thus although these students may be as intellectually capable as their academic-track peers, they find themselves in low-status, low-achieving vocational or general-track courses because they failed to measure up in their previous year's academic work. Furthermore, the tournament system that prevails in secondary schools typically offers only one opportunity: once a student is placed in a lower track, he or she very rarely moves up from that level.

The Cooling-Out Model

Finally, the cooling-out model emphasizes the functional importance to society of hierarchical track arrangements in reserving scarce and well-paying jobs for the few persons assigned to high-powered academic classes. The "heated-up" aspirations of those who have not been placed consistently in high-track or honors courses during their school careers must be cooled down in order to preserve the orderly flow of workers into lower-status jobs. Like the economic and the tournament models, the cooling-out perspective emphasizes the significance of curricular track placement in predicting occupational futures after school. This model, however, is unique in employing the metaphor of the holding pen. Attending school, especially while enrolled in courses in the general track, restrains students who are potentially rebellious or who are a threat to the job status of adults, particularly those who have families to support. Students' rebelliousness and job aspirations are cooled out for a period of years until youths are considered to be of suitable age to enter the labor market.

Although these four models vary, the determinist position overall emphasizes the close correspondence between social relations and rewards in school and at work through the allocation of a few highly favored slots in the academic track and in the occupational structure. Moreover, the process of allocating scarce and highly prized slots is relentlessly mechanistic; it reflects a general societal bias against poor, and Hispanic, and African-American students. The system contains very little room for "play"; students move in lockstep from their studies in school to prescribed positions in the world of work. Thus although the determinist position is useful in identifying *structures*, such as tracking arrangements in high school, it is not helpful in analyzing the *processes* by which individuals are sorted into particular curricular trenches and subsequently into particular occupations.

THE CULTURAL CAPITAL PERSPECTIVE

In contrast to the various determinist positions, the cultural capital perspective underscores the benefits to the elite and the costs to the nonelite of cultural baggage distributed in the family and the school rather than emphasizing the mechanistic workings of status allocation. However, Pierre Bourdieu and others who have made empirical tests of Bourdieu's theoretical work stress the importance of the status-attainment processes lurking behind visible cultural forms. Bourdieu's notion of "cultural capital" is strongly tied to social class and to the hierarchical ordering of knowledge-based systems in schools.

From our consideration of the process of status allocation in school, we know that students receive differential access to academic studies and consequently acquire different types and amounts of cultural equipment. In Bourdieu's formulations, cultural capital refers to socially ratified instrumental knowledge, "gifts," and skills safeguarded and nurtured by the upper and upper-middle classes and used by them to maintain their hegemony in society (Bourdieu and Passeron 1977). In the language of those who adopt the strongly deterministic structural approaches, these skills and this knowledge would explain the percentage of variance unaccounted for in models of status mobility. Although nonelite social classes obviously also have a rich store of cultural patterns, such as language and musical tastes, they are not prized in a Eurocentric, racist, and sexist society such as ours (Lareau 1989). This arrangement carries an obvious payoff for the social class groups who are able to corner the cultural capital market and to preserve it for the benefit of their children. The establishment of elite schools, the mastery of particular forms of knowledge, and the adoption of new technologies are strategies used by the upper classes to perpetuate the social order (DiMaggio 1982; Persell and Cookson 1987).

Bourdieu emphasizes the importance of maintaining a

monopoly on cultural capital through a shared system of "internalized structures, schemes of perception, conception, and action common to all members of the same group or class" (Bourdieu and Passeron 1977, 86). This notion is summarized in the concept of "habitus," which refers to the social world of shared values, attitudes, beliefs, and behaviors of a particular class, although Bourdieu is concerned primarily with the cultural capital sanctioned by the elite, whose values and goals set the social standard. Thus our national system of schooling, based on a Eurocentric model, is grounded in the high value attached to the worldview of privileged groups in society. This view emphasizes academic education and makes school experience profoundly alienating to out-groups, particularly working class and nonwhite students. According to MacLeod (1987),

> the structure of schooling with its high regard for the cultural capital of the upper classes promotes a belief among working-class students that they are unlikely to achieve academic success. Thus, there is a correlation between objective probabilities and subjective aspirations, between institutional structures and cultural practices (3).

One of the most interesting empirical applications of Bourdieu's conceptions of cultural capital and habitus occurred in a recent study of computer use among students attending elite American boarding schools (Persell and Cookson 1987). In research conducted in field visits to forty-eight private secondary boarding schools and through surveys of 2,475 students, Persell and Cookson analyzed the extent to which schools had developed computer facilities on campus, the frequency with which students used computers, and the characteristics of frequent users. Not surprisingly, in view of Bourdieu's theory, the researchers found that computer facilities in these schools were housed in elaborate structures; many were built as separate wings or as adjacent buildings. Computers formed the centerpiece of the school curriculum; computer skills were regarded as critical for students who aspired to attend Ivy League schools.

At the time of the Persell and Cookson study, computer literacy was being established in elite colleges and universities as a requirement for admission to the freshman class; thus computer skills were becoming important cultural capital. Students who used computers frequently were more likely to see themselves as majoring in high-status science-related and technical fields in college. In addition, male students and Asian students were likely to use computers more often than white female students. In view of our society's premium on the development of technical skills among males, it is not surprising that facilities were more extensive in all-male schools and that more male students reported having computers at home. The habitus of upper-class males in American society, as Bourdieu's theory would predict, is more likely to foster high aspirations and strong ambitions in areas generally valued and rewarded by society, in this case sophisticated knowledge and skills in computer use.

Although the cultural capital perspective explores the shared values, norms, and behaviors of a particular class, actual social relationships among individuals in a specific milieu or habitus are more hinted at than described. Moreover, it is difficult to see the links among the major institutions that propel the individual from school to work. Finally, the cultural capital perspective emphasizes the value of a Eurocentric scheme of skills and tastes. It does not acknowledge that nonelite families possess cultural *resources* that constitute a rich store of experience virtually unrecognized by teachers and others (Lareau 1989).

THE SUBCULTURE PERSPECTIVE

In contrast to the vague picture painted by both cultural reproduction and cultural capital theories, the notion of "linguistic subculture" is useful in illustrating exactly how family, school, and work form a tightly linked chain that depends on socially shared knowledge rather than exclusively on cultural capital. According to this perspective, subcultures develop among individuals who are connected socially and who interact with one another regularly. Subcultural groups develop in families, classrooms, and workplaces. The interaction over time within subcultural groups leads to a commonly held system of values, patterns of thinking and acting, and particular forms of language, which together constitute socially shared knowledge.

Basil Bernstein (1975, 1977) has examined the formation of linguistic codes that distinguish different social class groups. Although we must be cautious not to equate subcultural groups with social class groups, our society values an elite core of cultural knowledge that incorporates a particular linguistic code. As an additional cautionary note let us keep in mind that Bernstein carried out his research in Britain, which is more highly stratified by class than is the United States. In essence, Bernstein's theory holds that working-class children develop highly context-dependent language patterns in their families. These children and their parents rely on the immediate setting to provide cues, and therefore produce a more restricted, more context-bound language code than do their middle-class counterparts. In contrast, middle-class parents use what Bernstein terms "an elaborated code" with a highly abstract set of meanings and (some scholars believe) a highly inflated syntax to accompany these meanings.

Although Melvin Kohn and his associates (1978, 1982, 1983) have not examined linguistic codes in the same manner as Bernstein has, they also are concerned with the way in which a worker's participation in a specific job-related subculture is linked to child-raising practices and subsequently to the child's orientation to school. In a series of studies Kohn determined that although working-class parents did not dampen their children's occupational ambitions, they tended to be more concerned with their children's outward appearance, "appropriate" sex role behavior, good manners, and conformance to parental authority. In contrast, middle-class parents tended to value their children's innovativeness, experimentation, and flexibility. Kohn has linked these different patterns of parental child-rearing values to the system of authority and the nature of work in jobs typically held by working-class and middle-class males. Working-class men experience authoritarian relations with bosses at work. Moreover, their jobs in industrial settings give a fragmented view of work and of the labor process. This view leads to their alienation from the workplace, a "gift" that they pass along to their children. In contrast, middle-class managers and professional workers enjoy considerably more autonomy on the job, tend to have more control over the work process, and generally are engaged with work that they consider meaningful. Subsequently they incorporate these values into their child-rearing strategies.

Thus language codes and accompanying child-rearing practices are rooted in the division of labor and can be observed in the patterns of authority and social control that exist in workplaces and in families. These patterns also exist in schools. The capacity to reason abstractly, the ability to express ideas in complex written and oral language, and the desire to innovate and experiment are all valued highly in school. These qualities are linked to curricular track placement in high school; academic-track students generally are perceived as possessing them. The relationship between social class and track placement is by no means cast in stone. Institutional career structures, however, are linked strongly to the social construction of ability in ways that favor middle-and upper-middle-class students in American schools (Rosenbaum 1986). Therefore, although the subcultural perspective is useful in explaining the school careers of particular groups of people, it fails to illustrate how some individuals are able to resist the seemingly inexorable influence of particular patterns of socialization experienced in the family and/or at school. This is principally because data representing middle-class or working-class orientations are considered in the aggregate. Individual cases grounded in a close examination of school-based or workplace behavior are not considered, limiting the extent to which linkages between culture and social structure can be examined (Epstein, 1990).

THE INDIVIDUAL PERSPECTIVE

In recent years a new way of understanding individual agency has been developed by cultural reproduction theorists. "Individual agency" refers to the individual's capacity to resist, conform, or take a compromising stance in relation to social structure. In a model of status attainment, these individual actions would be seen as intervening variables, "variously described as 'passive obedience and loyalty' learned in school" (Bowles and Gintis 1976) or as coping strategies that individuals use to confront problems encountered routinely in organizations, such as "retreatism, ritualistic conformity, innovation and rebellion" (Corwin and Namboodiri 1989). In a recent ethnography of schooling that examined coping strategies, Claus (1986) noted that reluctant students in a vocational education class could resist authority by inducing their classmates and the teacher to complete their class projects, thus demonstrating their considerable skill in manipulating the system.

Individual agency should not be equated with isolated, autonomous behavior, especially in the case of peer-oriented youths in the context of school classrooms. Such youths are likely to act in concert with others who occupy similar cultural and social positions such as the students in the vocational class described by Claus. The useful aspect of a focus on individual agency seems to be the emphasis on the conscious realization that individuals do have choices. The limiting aspect seems to be that in the case of the vocational students in Claus's research and in the other examples to be reviewed here, choices are made from among culturally and socially established options. Individuals may alter or change these options, but they do so primarily in stylistic rather than substantive terms (Hammack 1988).

Sociologists in the old functionalist days regarded students' resistance behaviors as acts of deviance. Now, rather romantically, the student rebel or the nonconformist young worker is seen by such theorists as Willis (1977), Giroux (1981), and others (but generally not by teachers or employers) as a Robin Hood or a Luke Skywalker, heroically confronting the evil sheriffs and Darth Vaders of authoritarianism and class domination.

In both earlier and more recent formulations of the individual perspective, the cultural milieu is viewed as the mediating influence on individual behavior; in turn, social class structures are the dominating force affecting the cultural milieu. The most widely discussed and most influential research in this tradition is Paul Willis's (1977) ethnography of "the lads," a particularly alienated but (according to Willis) politically astute group of working-class youths attending a British comprehensive high school. Willis's account argues consistently against a determinist or reductionist view of the lads' behaviors, values, and beliefs. The lads are portrayed as "constructing their own world in a way which is recognizably human and not theoretically reductive" (Willis 1977, 171). Moreover, as a conscious act of rebellion they elect to "have a laff" rather than to accept passively the school culture. Their resistance to the culture of the passive "ear'oles" develops as a result of their "partial penetrations" into the structures of economic domination.

Unfortunately, the lads' "insights" into the structures of class oppression are limited by their unalloyed racist and sexist attitudes and behaviors. The lads value manual labor in shop-floor jobs both because they see these jobs as allowing time to "have a laff" and because they view mental work as feminized. It is difficult to accept Willis's position that the lads possess sufficient insight into the nature of capitalist structures, with their overlays of paternalism and racism, to function as catalysts for a coming social revolution.

Nonetheless, Willis's research has had powerfully persuasive effects on theories and research on the relationship between school and work among those who emphasize individual agency. For example, Peter McLaren's (1986) study of working-class Anglo and Portuguese students attending a Canadian parochial school celebrates the significance of individual agency in the context of repressive school practices. Like Willis's study, McLaren's research is important in showing that working-class schools do not produce docile, passive learners. Both Willis and McLaren demonstrate that class and cultural capital are hardly static concepts with little role in social relations and individual action. Yet, without a better understanding of the actual levels of intellectual and political awareness possessed by the students under study, it is premature to regard students' "acts of resistance" as sophisticated counterhegemonic strategies pregnant with political meaning (Giroux 1983).

Moreover, blatant sexism surely must be explained rather than displayed as illustrative of students' resistance. Henry Giroux is a leading cultural reproduction theorist who has taken an individual perspective in his lively and powerful syntheses of empirical work by Willis, McLaren, and others. Yet, like the researchers whose work he obviously admires, Giroux appears to view male adolescents' raging ambivalence toward women as a manifestation of their political resistance to authority. He uses the following passage from McLaren's research to illustrate students' rebelliousness:

Let's have art this afternoon, Mr. McLaren!
Yah. We want art!
Well, we've got some math to do this afternoon, perhaps after we've finished with that . . .
We wanna naked model . . . one with really big tits that stick out to here! . . . and lots of fuzzy hair down here!
You guys are sick! Is that all you think about?
Shut up Sandra! All you think about is naked boys!
Barry's a fag. He thinks about naked boys too! . . .
Sir! Let's have floor hockey instead!
I hates floor hockey!
We don't want you girls! Hey, sir! Let the girls play skippin or somethin, but let us play floor hockey!
There will be no playing anything until we finish our math.
Kids should be allowed to choose sometimes. You said so!
Yah! You never let us have fun—real fun!
Okay, okay. What does "real fun" mean?
If we wanna go somewheres, the creek or somethin, they say you should let us . . .
. . . Open your books to the math review on page fifty-one.
Wait a minute! I ain't gots no pencil!
That's because you used it to jab that little kid at recess and the teacher took it off you!

Get lost . . .
Here you can use my pencil.
Thanks, sir! Hey look! I stole the teacher's pencil!
Can I turn on the radio during art?
Quietly, yes . . . quietly. But first, our math!
Hey Sandra, get up on the desk and take off your shirt!
Anybody who doesn't finish this test gets a note to take
    home and get signed.
Sir! Can I have a note, please! I love notes!
Me too! I wanna note saying I'm bad!
Everybody line up for bad notes!
    . . . Hey! Gimme back my math book!
Cut the crap!
This is boring . . . (Giroux, p. 95–96)

This passage contains strongly phrased utterances of male rage directed toward the young women in the classroom. This rage remains unchallenged both by the teacher (McLaren) and by the researcher (Giroux), who quotes this passage in admiration of what he sees as political resistance.

To Giroux's credit, he is critical of theories of resistance in part because they fail to address gender issues adequately. His summary statement is clear on this point: "The failure to include women and minorities of color in such studies has resulted in a rather uncritical theoretical tendency to romanticize modes of resistance even when they contain reactionary views about women" (Giroux 1983, 105). Cultural reproduction theory focused on individual agency, however, must do more than wag a finger at gender bias.

In their favor, studies such as those of Willis and McLaren illuminate the complexity of social reproduction in schools and workplaces. These studies do not consider the status attainment process to be the outcome of secondary school and societal characteristics interacting with students' characteristics in a deterministic fashion, as in the structural determinist models. Instead they illustrate the roles played by students themselves in constructing a class- and gender-based culture and work identity. Most of these studies, however, have been weakened by their lack of attention to gender issues.

Feminist Perspectives

More sobering, if less colorful, individual theories of social and cultural reproduction are emerging in the work of feminist scholars. These observers are less eager than Willis, Giroux, McLaren, and others to celebrate the picaresque cultural worlds of rebellious male students or to view adolescents' racist and sexist acts as heroic strategies of resistance to economic oppression. Most research on the relationship between school and work has been based on men's experience. Women have been studied less both because male researchers are less interested in women and because women have been viewed as girlfriends, wives, and mothers rather than as serious participants in the work force (Gaskell 1986, 2).

Three notable exceptions are the ethnographies of Jane Gaskell (1986), Linda Valli (1986), and Christine Griffin (1985). Each of these scholars argues that gender issues must receive attention equal to that given to social class. Therefore each focuses explicitly on young women's experiences in training to take jobs as clerical workers, in the retail trades, and in pink-collar jobs. In addition, these accounts are particularly clear in their focus on young women's domestic commitments: they emphasize the important influences of romantic love and the family on females' transition from school to work (Holland and Eisenhart, 1990).

These studies produce several important conclusions about the role of individual agency in young women's lives. First, it is clear that vocational classrooms reproduce the workplace in significant ways. Despite employers' concerns about the inadequacy of vocational preparation in school, the students *are* exposed to skills required by the job markets they are likely to enter. Valli's detailed analysis of the clerical skills taught in schools demonstrates that these skills ranged from filing to word processing and accounting. (Students uniformly preferred jobs that required the most difficult skills.) Second, instructors and instruction are remote from the actual world of work because instructors must rely on their own (often distant) contact with the workplace, visits with employers, readings, and contact with former students (Gaskell 1986). Most of the students in Gaskell's study held extremely negative views of school, describing it as "boring and useless." Somewhat naively they believed that they had "chosen" not to strive in school and that they were not smart enough to go on in school. Virtually all were extremely enthusiastic about obtaining work, although subsequently they experienced dissatisfaction with jobs that exhibited the negative characteristics associated with employment in the youth labor market (e.g., low wages, low skill demands, high turnover). Conformance rather than rebellion appears to be the norm for young women whose individual agency is restricted severely by structural inequities in job opportunities, wages, and mobility in their decisions about school and work.

One year after graduation, most of Gaskell's subjects regretted the decision to find work rather than continuing their education. Most reported that they would return to school if they could; that they wished they had performed better while in school and had been told about the consequences of the decision to leave school for work. Many subjects cited school-related factors as influencing their ill-informed choices. In this regard school counselors drew the heaviest criticism. They were blamed for not letting students take enough academic courses, particularly in science, and for not providing adequate information about work generally. On the positive side, these youths viewed work as contributing distinct material and social advantages, enhancing their financial well-being, and bringing them independence from parents.

Gaskell and Lazerson (1980–81) noted an array of gender differences related to attitudes toward work. Boys were more likely than girls to view their current employment situations as temporary: in this way they reduced the impact of their current jobs on their self-image. Boys also planned to move on to better jobs either by job shopping or by returning to school. Girls, on the other hand, were more satisfied with their decisions overall and saw work itself as temporary; they assumed that marriage soon would terminate their commitment to work. Gaskell and Lazerson fault society for its benign portrayal of the economic system and for perpetuating the myth that energetic job-seekers locate good jobs. In reality, job changes for working-class youths are typically horizontal, and young women, though they may leave work temporarily, return after childbirth. More important, Gaskell and Lazerson assert that the potentially most valuable feature of school is precisely what is missing from jobs. Literacy, critical awareness, and exposure to new ideas, which are what education ought to be about, are not what these young persons' jobs are about (Gaskell and Lazerson 1980, 94).

In her analysis of the reproduction of the clerical labor force, Valli determined that young women are both bound and liberated by particular "structural, ideological and cultural elements" (Valli 1986, 197). Valli's study took place over the course of a year at "Woodrow High School" in "Macomb," a midwestern city of approximately 200,000. Her analyses considered the methods by which students were selected into the Cooperative Office Education Program (COOP), the extent to which students themselves selected this course of study, the nature of the technical skills taught in the cur-

riculum, the characteristics of exchange, authority, and gender relations in the office work curriculum, and related workplace experiences for the young women enrolled in the program.

The results of Valli's study failed to confirm major assumptions of economic, gatekeeping, tournament, or cooling-out models
to explain the allocation of students to the COOP program. First,
virtually any student who applied to the program was accepted.
Second, most students appeared to have stumbled on the program
rather than having been recruited into it. Lack of information, a
student-to-counselor ratio of 400 to 1, and the perception that
women did not have to "settle" for positions as clerical workers in
an era of expanded employment opportunities combined to limit
enrollment to twenty-seven students during the year (1980–81) of
the study. According to Valli, young women selected themselves
into the COOP curriculum primarily because their commonsense
notions both about their life course as wives and mothers and about
the nature of "appropriate" women's work made office work the
most attractive alternative. Even though some of the program participants had aspired to pursue college degrees in accounting, biolo-
gy, and other fields, office work was perceived in the end as

> a sensible safeguard against unemployment or employment
> in even less desirable positions. Office preparation was a sen-
> sible accommodation to a work world that was limited either
> by views of what was appropriate or desirable for a woman or
> of what was possible for a woman (Valli 1986, 78).

Work tasks included in school-based training were not uniformly
vacuous, low in skill requirements, or boring, although not all of the
skills taught in the classroom were demanded at COOP work sites.
During their course of study, students were taught filing, typing, pho-
tocopying, and record keeping; later they used these skills in their
cooperative jobs. Their skill and knowledge levels, however, surpassed the demands of the work they carried out; as a result, they
were "dissatisfied and unchallenged." The most satisfied workers
were those whose job placements allowed them to use the more complex skills of advanced typing, editing, word processing, and accounting, and in which they were rotated routinely among various tasks,
held a number of roles simultaneously, and frequently encountered
the public or used a variety of skills (Valli 1986, 191–92).

Valli's study demonstrates the strength of social representa-
tions of gendered work in limiting girls' occupational choices.

Occupational aims, hopes, and expectations play a comparatively unimportant role in girls' plans for the future. Other research (West and Newton 1983) amplifies these findings by noting the following:

> During the adolescent years when girls' academic interests decline, the range of occupations chosen by girls also narrows. The social pressures on adolescent girls to aspire to sex-appropriate occupations and to relinquish ambitious, achievement-oriented career plans are undoubtedly strong (179).

Initial choice of jobs requiring "inappropriate" sex role behaviors may be discouraged by family, friends, the media, or girls' views of the trajectories of their own life courses. Valli, however, cautions that the simple notion that mobility or status attainment guides career choices for all adolescents may be dramatically misinformed, and may reflect middle-class concerns with career development and mobility. The notion of individual agency enriches cultural reproduction theory by showing forcefully through empirical research that people do exercise choice and that processes of cultural reproduction are neither static nor mechanistic. The notion has been flawed, however, by a romantic emphasis on male deviance and by a view that appears to celebrate racist and sexist behaviors as somehow heroic and even politically sophisticated acts of resistance. In order to formulate a fully fledged individual perspective on the transition from school to work, we must consider variation within groups of individuals. As we have seen among young women, not only does their choice of curricular options in high school reflect a capacity for agency; in addition their interest in interpersonal relationships, family formation, and romantic love must be taken into account, as illustrated in Valli's study. Valli's study of the school-to-work transition for girls enrolled in a high school clerical course highlights the importance of gender in any analysis of the effects of curricular program choice, job experience, and occupational plans. Gender as well as other social factors, in addition to social class, profoundly effect curricular placement in school and subsequent job outcomes.

SCHOOL VERSUS WORK

The debate over the benefits and costs of working at jobs outside the classroom while in school or of leaving school for work is hardly resolved, largely because social and behavioral scientists have tended to ignore work-related issues that are paramount for adolescents during this period in their lives.

One of these issues, forging an identity, includes struggling with components of self-identity that focus on a definition (or definitions) of oneself as a paid or an unpaid worker. These definitions vary by gender, race, and ethnicity, and other social characteristics.

Economists stress the general finding that holding a job while in school reduces later unemployment and increases post-school hourly wages of both black and white youths. Sociologists and psychologists, however, argue that working while in school or leaving school for work constrains youths' possibilities for pursuing other opportunities such as participation in sports and the enjoyment of leisure time. Leading advocates of this position are Greenberger and her colleagues (1981, 1986), who argue strongly for a moratorium on work during the high school years to allow youths to pursue leisure activities, to concentrate on schoolwork, and to develop interests through participation in school-and community-based activities. Research in the psychiatric literature supports the view that youth benefit from unfettered free time (Csikszentmihalyi and Larson 1984). Such time allows youths a moratorium in the process of identity formation and is an extremely middle-class notion.

Most of the research arguing for a moratorium from such "adult" pursuits as working during adolescence reflects the interests and concerns of middle-class, suburban populations participating in these studies and possibly reveals the biases of the researchers conducting them. In fact, one of the greatest barriers to planning programs for increasing opportunities for access to Eurocentric cultural capital in secondary school is the phenomenon of social and cultural reproduction, which allows social relations, including relations in leisure pursuits as well as in work, to be perpetuated from one generation to the next. Why not a moratorium for all youths regardless of socioeconomic status? The reality, however, is the dilemma of disadvantaged youths whose material circumstances do not provide the environmental benefits enjoyed by their middle- and upper-middle-class counterparts (Clark 1983).

The disparities between resource-rich and resource-poor environments and their effects on young people are illustrated in a study by Heyns (1978); she found that advantaged children continued to learn throughout the out-of-school summer months, at least as measured by their performance on achievement tests. Their economically disadvantaged counterparts, however, failed to gain materially from their summer experiences, and in fact were likely to suffer a decline in performance. During the school year, these groups of children displayed similar rates of learning; this finding suggests the importance of enhancing disadvantaged children's skill development during the summer months. Burbridge (1985) and others have suggested that summer employment programs coupled with school-related instruction may prove to be the best idea for many youths, particularly for the disadvantaged. This suggestion resonates well with Heyns's findings.

There are compelling reasons to believe that such programs will work especially well for this target group. In many instances, disadvantaged youths work because they must and because they wish to possess those things that middle-class children are given but do not really need. In fact, in the absence of summer employment or part-time employment during the school year, youths from poor families are likely to drop out of school permanently to seek full-time employment. From the programmatic side, policy initiatives that focus exclusively on employability issues do so because such programs are easier to conduct than programs aimed at raising a teenager's seventh-grade reading skills to a twelfth-grade level during summer school or in after-school instructional programs (Hahn and Lerman 1985). It is even more difficult to develop a work slot for a student in a challenging job as well as connect what goes on at the job to what is being learned in the classroom (Corwin 1986).

Yet, it is precisely these experiences and opportunities, together with an understanding of the inequities inherent in American occupational structures, that programs need to emphasize and that many youths wish to acquire rather than character development and resume writing. Unfortunately, curriculum focused on employability issues alone has dominated such national programs as Jobs for America's Graduates (Borman and Reisman 1986).

YOUTH AS A PHASE

Because youth is a phase of life that encompasses a unique set of factors affecting all aspects of young people's lives, including occupational identity, issues related to youth and adolescence have clear and obvious implications for the school-to-work transition. In addition, major cyclical and structural factors inherent in the economic and labor market spheres of American society are particularly obdurate. They resist alterations even by well-designed and comprehensive programs to facilitate the school-to-work transition. In chapter 2 we will examine labor market conditions for youths in the United States. First, however, we will consider the period of youth itself, because of its implications for the relationship between school and work.

Marsland (1987) and others argued recently for an analysis of youth as a sociological construct. Although this idea may seem trivial to our considerations here, I believe it is valuable for at least two compelling reasons.

First, during the 1970s and 1980s, liberal and Marxist critics emphasized the primacy of social class in fully, not partially, explaining issues related to unemployment, delinquency, and school failure. All of these issues, not coincidentally, are popularly associated with the period of adolescence and youth. These analysts, particularly the Marxists, argued that societal culture is defined by dominant class concerns, which in turn influence youth subcultures overwhelmingly (Brake 1980). Subsequently, they trivialized or ignored critical features of adolescence as a period in the life course, such as idealism coupled with political naiveté. We can see evidence of this perspective in the cultural reproduction theories as exemplified in the works of individual theorists such as Willis. These works dismiss any notion of a viable youth culture with a set of core values and orientations developing from a perspective shared by the young, which is separate from either a working-class or a middle-class ideology.

Gender and (to some extent) race and ethnicity also were regarded in these analyses as trivial in defining youths' experiences. Any problem encountered by youths entering the labor market was viewed as the result of exploitative conditions characteristic of a capitalist economy rather than as an interaction between labor market conditions and individual characteristics such as gender, race, and ethnicity. In this intellectual atmosphere, the position taken by Willis and others made good sense. Male students, as we have seen in Willis's and McLaren's accounts, could be viewed easily as self-consciously resisting authority in a politically sophisticated manner. Charges of racism and sexism leveled at their behavior could be dismissed in favor of a focus on social class and on external exploitative conditions. Apologists such as Giroux could argue that the pressures of working-class culture "made them do it."

Second, youth as a period in the life course has been ignored by sociologists, who believe that to do otherwise is to engage in reductionist, psychological thinking (Marsland 1987). Yet in discarding theories that focus on the individual and the self, sociologists, with few exceptions, have been left with poor explanatory frameworks for such issues as job hopping, which particularly characterizes the work experience of the young. One could explain why youths change jobs frequently (averaging less than nine months in a particular job) by asserting that all jobs in American society lack challenge and exploit the workers who hold them. This assertion may be true in part—many jobs are inherently without challenge—but the question still remains: Why do young workers change jobs far more frequently than older workers? It appears that this phenomenon cannot be explained fully by referring only to job characteristics. In addition, dimensions of youth as a phase in the life course from the perspective of a sociology of youth must be included in any thorough explanation of the relationship between school and work, of school policy, and of other related matters.

The most important aspect of a sociology of youth in connection with the school-to-work transition seems to be Erikson's (1950) notion of occupational identity. Erikson argued that changes in occupational identity during adolescence are congruent with adolescents' growing independence from authority figures. These alterations in identity are tempered by and interact with young workers' experiences in the labor market. In view of the nature of many job options available to youths, it may be most adaptive to adopt a strategy of job hopping during the early phases of the school-to-work transition. Certainly, decisions to seek different forms of work are generally easier for younger than for older workers; this observation suggests that individuals during this period in the life course are particularly resilient and flexible in their capacity to endure and even to seek different forms of work experience.

Erikson's perspective on identity formation has been elaborated by studies of adolescents' labor market experience. One important concept emerging from this research, as mentioned previously, is the notion of a "moratorium," a period of delay during adolescence when various social and work roles can be "tried on." The problem with this concept, in addition to its middle-class bias, is that the moratorium often is perceived as a floundering period in which adolescents are considered to be unskilled, defiant, and unready to assume responsibility.

In a recent report on the nation's "forgotten half," members of the William T. Grant Foundation's (1988) Commission on Work, Family, and Citizenship argue that the social construction of adolescence in the United States emphasizes the "pre-adult" status of young people. The result of this bias is a distorted view of youth as "in the process of preparing for life and not yet fully equipped to participate in it." In addition, adolescence has been viewed as a period of plasticity, during which many youths are lured from the path of development as productive, directed, and responsible adults to deviance and criminal activity.

The tendency to see the young as characterized by their weaknesses rather than by their strengths has been reflected in public policies and in attitudes of employers (and others) toward young people. The Grant Commission argues that the group that suffers the most negative stereotyping consists of those who do not enroll in higher education programs after high school. Thus although youths value work and wish to become economically successful in terms of a middle-class standard, employers' perspective toward this group remains negative. This finding should not be surprising in light of the pervasive bias toward elite knowledge in American society. As a result of this bias, youths who seek employment rather than post-secondary education after leaving high school suffer "an extended floundering period in the labor market before beginning a real career." They do so as a result of employers' actions, adults' attitudes and expectations for their behavior, and the viability of local labor conditions, but *not* as a result of the "inherent characteristics of youth" (W.T. Grant Commission on Work, Family and Citizenship 1988, 26).

In fact, adolescents clearly value work. In their analysis of high school seniors participating in the 1982 High School and Beyond survey, Eckstrom and her colleagues (1989) examined responses to students' ratings of the importance to them of work, family, friendship, and other social relationships and activities. The five items rated as most important in their lives were, in order, success in work; marriage and family life; strong friendships; steady work; and better opportunities for their own children. The results of this analysis are somewhat ironic when one considers the unsavory view of adolescent workers that seems to be implicit in the limited range of opportunities to engage in meaningful work that is typically available to youths.

Several themes have emerged from my analyses of cultural reproduction theory, from a consideration of youths' transition from school to work, and from a discussion of the nature of youth as a social construct. I will pursue these themes in the analysis of young workers' day-to-day experiences in the workplace. Bourdieu's theory, for example, demonstrates the importance of the habitus of institutions in which social relations are shaped, such as the family, the school, and the workplace. This habitus is a key element in determining the extent to which young workers will acquire the skills, the values, and the experience they need to find work they consider meaningful and commensurate with their skills and interests. When we observe how workplace environments vary in the extent to which young workers view their own occupational identities as commensurate with their current activities, we gain insight into the fit between the individual and the environment in which he or she works.

Various cultural reproduction theories have attempted to explain the fit between social relations in the family and social relations in other institutions, particularly in school and at work. Similarly, theories of the transition from school to work have been developed in a wide array of disciplines. Chapter 1 has considered the impact of this transition primarily in connection with its effects on the individual young worker both from the perspective of sociology and (in a more limited way) from that of developmental psychology.

The two perspectives to be considered next in chapter 2 are those of economics and sociology. Economic theories emphasize the importance of labor markets in determining where students will work once they leave school and what forces will lead to their employment or unemployment. Sociological theories stress the importance of the work organization and culture in shaping youths' experiences.

2. LABOR MARKET, STRUCTURAL, AND ORGANIZATIONAL ISSUES IN MOVING FROM SCHOOL TO WORK

CHAPTER 1 FOCUSED ON the relationship between school and work, emphasizing the cultural reproduction of individuals as they move from the influence of one social sphere to the next. More often than not people remain in overlapping spheres, such as family and work settings. Explaining the reproduction of social relationships and the perpetuation of social and economic arrangements across generations was a primary aim of the perspectives considered in chapter 1.

In contrast, the prevailing large-scale or macro social perspective on youths' transition from school to work, which is examined in the current chapter, emphasizes the fit between *youths' labor market capital*—their skills, talents, and abilities—and *labor market demands* for their work-related efforts (Borman and Hopkins 1987). Historically, such analyses have emphasized the demand side—the specific skills, attitudes, and background experiences that employers desire in young workers. In this chapter I acknowledge the contribution of economic labor market theory to understanding current conditions that affect both young men and young women, especially when they are seeking access to jobs, are being evaluated on the job and are attempting to gain better opportunities. Then I move on to a consider the importance of social organizational theory in sociology for a thorough analysis of workplace conditions, particularly task technology, the workplace authority structure and the job reward distribution system, which constrain young workers' experience. Finally I begin to describe the observational case studies that are examined in the remainder of the book.

Although generally it places more emphasis on the demand side, *economic theory* related to the transition from school to work considers both the characteristics of young workers (the supply side) and the attributes of the youth labor market (the demand side). In addition it attempts to explain how supply and demand mesh to result both in successful job shopping for young job seekers and in relatively low rates of unemployment for society, or to explain how the reverse occurs. *Sociological theory* is more inclined to consider such aspects of the school-to-work transition as talent matching —the degree to which young workers' skills and attitudes harmonize with employers' needs—and socialization—the extent to which the worker accommodates to the workplace. Also of interest to sociologists is the effect of the organizational milieu on the young worker. In this context, patterns of authority, the occupational structure of youths' jobs, and the system of rewards, job responsibilities, social interaction, and other organizationally dependent variables are particularly important in demonstrating the dynamic role of the workplace in young workers' lives. In the two sections of the chapter that follow immediately, I will examine both of these perspectives.

THE YOUTH LABOR MARKET

In labor market economics as in any field, a range of assumptions guides explanations of how youths' abilities, education, and other attributes connect with jobs. Two positions govern the thinking in this area: orthodox economic theory and segmented labor market theory (Miller 1981).

Orthodox economic theorists portray the school-to-work transition in rather simple terms, guided by three basic assumptions. First, there is only one labor market in society, in which all members of the society compete for jobs. Second, the marketplace operates in a rational and competitive manner. Those most fit for jobs receive them; discrimination and employers' bias recede in their influence on the meshing between workers' skills and labor market demands. Third, neither workers nor employers are influenced by bias, subjectivity, or irrational impulses as they make plans and decisions concerning employment. Thus, according to this explanation, the maid who works in a hotel and the person who works in a car wash are both paid low wages because their work tasks are so simple that almost anyone in the society can carry them out. Therefore, employers need not pay higher wages to find workers (Miller 1981, 289).

Conversely, heart surgeons receive extremely high salaries because their training is so demanding, their skills so scarce, and their talent so badly needed in society that their rewards should be and are indeed high. This characterization of the labor market emphasizes balance, harmony, and the generally benign aspects of the school-to-work transition.

One problem with this perspective is that the assumptions on which it is constructed promote policies and attitudes that limit reform efforts to federal, state, and locally assisted programs. Such programs provide training of limited scope because it is assumed that most people do not have the abilities or the desire to become heart surgeons, lawyers, college professors, and the like. Viewing those who are underemployed or unemployed as trainable only for low-level jobs promotes programs such as those mentioned in chapter 1, which emphasize résumé writing and interview skills. This is lean cultural capital indeed.

Segmented labor market theory presents a more sophisticated view of how workers locate and fit into jobs. According to this theory, the labor market is divided into at least two major segments; each operates with its own set of principles governing access, rewards, opportunities for promotion, and the like (Doeringer and Piore 1971). One segment is the primary or institutionalized labor market, which contains well-paying jobs, a career ladder internal to the work organization, and an evaluation of performance on the job in terms of clear criteria for evaluation (Miller 1981). In contrast, positions held by individuals in the secondary labor market have few advantages: jobs are low-paying; hours are irregular and/or part time; there is little or no opportunity for advancement, and although evaluation might appear to be "objective" because of the employer's use of rating sheets, it is influenced by the informal social relations between employer and employee in the work setting.

In orthodox labor market theory, workers obtain better jobs through competition by selling their skills in an open, rational market. According to segmented labor market theory, the major institutional arrangement governing the process of gaining a job must be understood in terms of the concept of "job shelters."

Job shelters or work reservations are created and maintained by discriminatory employment patterns. According to Miller (1981),

> modern labor markets are not based on pure competition; rather, they operate to discriminate against women, some ethnic and racial minorities, the young, the old, and others who have not received equal treatment historically or have been made superfluous by recent changes in technology. Labor market segmentation, then, stems purely from the past efforts of employers to encourage ethnic, sexual and other forms of competition and antagonism among workers in order to better control them and to keep wages low (292–93).

In addition to these arrangements of clear benefit to both employers and middle-class workers, monopolization of good jobs through the development of job shelters arises over time through the creation of assumptions about the "necessary" traits and behaviors for specific jobs. Thus, in the appliance repair store that employed Peter, one of the participants in the study, the employers assumed that white males, preferably those who had graduated from parochial rather than vocational schools, made the best repairmen. Others were not even considered when a job opening occurred. In this organization, appliance-repair jobs were reserved for white males; so were all other positions in the firm except that of secretary, which was reserved for a white female.

Other methods for sheltering jobs are more rational and less overtly discriminatory. For example, labor unions may restrict membership and thus also may curb access to jobs in particular business organizations. The credentialing process, including licensure practices and diploma granting, also restricts access. Most employers in the youth labor market want to restrict job opportunities to those who have earned a high school diploma. In fact, wage rates generally are determined by the fact that a particular employee has a high school degree and not by specific competencies in (for example) mathematics or science.

Segmented labor theory is useful for understanding practices in the modern labor market by illustrating the ways in which labor markets are by no means free and unrestricted, but it is limited in its ability to explain the relationships that people develop with their work. Certainly jobs in the secondary labor market carry fewer benefits and opportunities than jobs in primary markets; it is also true, however, that the full range of jobs in the secondary labor market is

as vast as (presumably) peo[   ]ller
(1981) points out, "Segment~~ed labo~~   ⌐9 ~   ,er-sim-
plify the diverse social realities of modern work by reducing all
work experiences to a few variables, such as level of income and job
security" (296). To move beyond these limitations, it is imperative
to consider the daily work lives of a number of young workers and to
do so in the context of an approach that is sensitive to these matters.

In order to understand the school-to-work transition from the
perspective of labor market economics as it applies to youth, we
turn again to the 1985 high school cohort mentioned briefly at the
outset of chapter 1. According to the Bureau of Labor Statistics
(1986), about 1.1 million members of the class of 1985 did not enroll
in college. Approximately 82 percent of this group entered the labor
force. Participation rates were higher for men than for women.
Rates for African-Americans and Hispanics were lower than for
whites. Although the economic picture in 1985 was more favorable
than during the recession years earlier in the decade, one in four of
all persons attempting to enter the labor force was looking for work,
compared with one in six during the 1970s. Unemployment
remains relatively high among young workers, even though their
numbers are shrinking. Terminating education before high school
graduation is disadvantageous to youths in the American marketplace, in which employers increasingly demand better-educated
workers (Carnoy and Levin 1985). This may be the case because
workers overall are better educated and because a surplus of job
seekers holding college degrees exists in some fields, such as the
behavioral sciences. In other words, young workers incur a persistent cost under current labor market conditions: the demand side is
better able to call the shots by articulating particular employer
needs, such as maintaining low wages, than is the supply side;
young people still must attempt to sell their skills in the market.

When we look more closely at individual employers' hiring
decisions, it becomes quite clear that those who hire young workers hold certain expectations for their future job performance and
for related attitudes and behaviors. In his recent review of fourteen
studies examining employers' needs and their expectations for
newly hired young workers in a variety of jobs, Gary Natriello
(1987) concluded the following:

> The strongest trend in the results of these studies is the impor-
> tance employers place on employee attitudes . . . [such as career
> goals, enthusiasm for the job, desire to learn, and desire to

advance]. In 11 of the 14 studies [reviewed by Natriello] respondents cited the importance of proper attitudes among employees. The three studies in which attitudes were not cited focused only on basic skills. A second theme in these studies is the emphasis on basic skills as opposed to job specific skills. Employers were particularly interested in communication skills and problemsolving skills. Finally,employers also placed emphasis on an understanding of the work or business environment (6).

Although specific employer needs for entry-level workers were clear and consistent across all the studies that he reviewed, Natriello is extremely cautious about generalizing on the basis of the findings from these studies. The principal reason for his hesitancy in advocating policy at the school level congruent with employers' desires is the lack of a developed rationale in these and other related studies for cultivating some characteristics among employees and excluding others. In Natriello's words, "Conclusions phrased in terms of what employers find most problematic in new workers may have as much to do with the traits they were asked to comment on as with their true needs" (7).

There is an even more compelling reason to regard these findings with skepticism. Although studies such as those reviewed by Natriello reveal an association between various cognitive and noncognitive attributes of workers and their subsequent job performance, researchers and employers alike currently lack a clear understanding of how specific job contexts affect workplace performance in interaction with particular worker traits. Job contexts are complex; they comprise the web of influences on the young worker of such workplace conditions as task technology, the workplace authority structure, and the job reward system mentioned at the outset of this chapter. The job context is the site for social interaction in the workplace; it is the workplace habitus where the young worker develops both an image of himself or herself as a worker and an image of the work environment in which she or he is situated.

Once youths have been screened and hired by employers, their dependence on market demands does not end. The relative disadvantage to youths entering the labor market is illustrated clearly by the wages they earn and the jobs they hold. Currently there is discussion in Congress concerning the upgrading of the minimum wage. As of this writing the federal minimum wage stands at $3.35 per hour, the level it reached in January, 1981 under an amendment to the 1977 Fair Labor Standards Act.

According to Current Population Survey (CPS) data, in 1986 approximately 3.5 million workers earned the minimum wage, while an additional 1.6 million earned less per hour. These numbers are smaller than those for 1981, when 7.8 million workers' earnings were at or below the minimum. Not surprisingly, the great bulk of workers earning $3.35 per hour or less are aged sixteen to twenty-four years (Mellor 1987). In fact, 60 percent of minimum-wage earners belonged to this age group in 1986. Among teenagers alone (those aged sixteen to nineteen) the proportion of workers earning $3.35 or less was 32 percent in that year, a far higher level than for any other age group. Among employed persons aged thirty-five to fifty-four, for example, the proportion whose wages fell into this category had declined to a mere 4 percent.

Of course, earnings are related to other factors as well, such as race/ethnicity, education, gender, and geographic region. Thus, young workers were more likely to earn the minimum wage or less if they were African-American or Hispanic than if they were white (10 percent as opposed to 8.6 percent). Likewise, only 2 percent of those with four years of college earned the minimum wage, whereas 10 percent of workers over the age of twenty-five with eight years of education or less fell into this category. Altogether, workers who had not completed high school accounted for almost two-fifths of those workers above age twenty-five whose hourly wage was $3.35 or less (Mellor 1987, 35). Finally, white and Hispanic women were twice as likely as white men to earn the minimum wage or less, and all young workers living in the South were most likely to earn salaries in this range.

If we consider only the wages, we can conclude that youth jobs are segregated at the low end of the opportunity structure. These jobs, much like the tracking system in schools, function to keep youths in a holding pen and to separate them from the higher-paying jobs held by those who are older but not necessarily more skilled or more capable. Youth jobs are low-paying. They are also situated, for the most part, in the secondary labor market. Accordingly they are characterized not only by low pay but also by part-time and irregular hours and by little opportunity for either advancement or skill development.

THE OCCUPATIONAL STRUCTURE OF YOUTH JOBS

The jobs that young workers hold are those jobs most likely to pay the minimum wage, as we have seen. For the most part, these are jobs in the expanding service sector of the secondary labor market, particularly in food service and in retail and personal service sales. Overall they account for half of all minimum-wage workers, including workers aged sixteen to twenty-four. Employment problems confronting youths have their origins both in the conditions of the economy as a whole and in the related overall rates of unemployment besetting the economy. In addition, youths traditionally have held jobs and occupations that are less attractive to older workers (Kett 1977).

How work is experienced at the individual level is contingent both upon conditions of the labor market as was discussed in the previous section and upon the occupational structure with its attendant institutional opportunities and constraints as I will point out in the remainder of this chapter. These latter considerations— the occupational structure and related institutional features—are of particular interest to the sociological analysis of youths' experiences in their first "real" jobs put forward in this volume. In addition, however, as becomes increasingly clear in an analysis of specific cases, cohort effects color the individual's perception of the range of opportunities and constraints offered to a particular generation of young workers. Finally, the young worker's negotiation of work roles, job tasks, and other claims must be viewed in interaction with the claims of managers and others in positions of authority. Thus, the ultimate goal of this chapter is to set forward a rubric for understanding institutional and environmental contexts influencing social interaction and the socialization of young workers in the workplace.

Since 1950 important historical shifts have occurred in the occupational structure of youth jobs. One is the decline in the number of youths employed as farm laborers, primarily because of increased mechanization and the consolidation of individually operated family farms. Between 1950 and 1970 the youths most affected by this trend were African-American males, particularly in the rural South. A persistent effect of this decline is the vacuum created by the lack of compensating growth in low-skilled nonagricultural work, which might have substituted for lost farm jobs. African-American youth unemployment remains a major problem largely because of labor market discrimination (Freeman and Holzer 1986). Another important trend since 1950 is the decline in the proportion of nonwhite female jobholders employed as private household workers. At least in this case, however, the trend has been compensated partly by a growth in clerical occupations.

In addition, it has become clear that amount (i.e., number of years) of education is related to the spectrum of occupations available to youth. At the time of the 1979 National Longitudinal Survey, when high school dropouts were compared to high school students, college students, and nonenrolled high school graduates, dropouts suffered the narrowest occupational opportunities in white-collar and skilled jobs. Among female high school students and graduates, 46 percent between the ages of fourteen and twenty-one at the time of the survey were employed in low-level clerical positions. Although education by itself influences job opportunities, gender interacts with years of schooling to determine these opportunities.

Another way of looking at the employment opportunity structure for youths is to consider the distribution of young workers in various industrial sectors. Overall, as has been noted, approximately 40 percent of working youths are employed in the service sector; most are engaged in retail sales including food service, the so-called burger or fast-food economy. Among female high school graduates, routine clerical work such as filing and sorting in banking, insurance, and related businesses may be characterized as relatively good opportunities, because these jobs are white collar, are clean, and offer the potential for career development. In reality, however, as we will see in chapter 4, working conditions governing these jobs (including the reward system, the scope of work, freedom from supervision, and other dimensions that contribute to workers' satisfaction) are absent even in relatively high-status clerical positions.

With this overview of labor market and occupational conditions for youths in mind, we focus next on the dilemmas and issues that confront young people who seek jobs in two specific urban labor markets.

CINCINNATI AND COLUMBUS: DETERMINANTS OF THE ORGANIZATIONAL MILIEU

In 1983, when the research on young workers reported here was begun, the United States was experiencing a recession. Specific regions and particular businesses were hit especially hard. Unemployment among young workers was worst in the urban northeast and midwest; the "rust belt" cities of Chicago, Cleveland, and Detroit were virtually under siege in attempting to keep their economies afloat. Terms such as *plant closings* and *deindustrial-*

ization became part of the nation's vocabulary. In contrast, Silicon Valley in California and industrial pockets in New England, particularly in the Boston area, enjoyed an economic boomlet on the crest of a new wave of high technology.

The cities of Columbus and Cincinnati in Ohio, one of the nation's most-urbanized states, fell somewhere between the rust belt cities and the coastal high-tech centers in the economic well-being and stability of their labor forces. Although jobs were not plentiful, both cities continued to expand economically during this period, largely because their labor markets were far more diversified than those of cities such as Detroit or Youngstown.

Cincinnati's economic life is dominated by several corporate giants headquartered there. Procter & Gamble is the city's largest employer. The University of Cincinnati, with an enrollment of 37,000 students, ranks second. Procter & Gamble products such as soap, toothpaste, and other consumer goods are considered necessities in today's society. There is little real foreign competition for these products because of Procter & Gamble's strength abroad; thus the economic base remains comparatively secure and contributes to the city's overall conservative, rather aloof corporate climate. Cincinnati is a Blue Book city, where families build traditions and stay on. Other family-owned firms headquartered there include the Lindner retail enterprises, Kroger's, Federated Department Stores, and Cincinnati Milacron, a diverse array of highly successful businesses.

Columbus, the state's capital, boasts of being the country's All-American city. Indeed, many product lines are test marketed there, and Columbus is the home of corporate headquarters for Wendy's, Rax, and several other fast-food chains. Its economy expanded even more dramatically than Cincinnati's during the first half of the 1980s. During this period Columbus developed a strong service-sector base not only in the "new" services, such as fast foods, but also in the more traditional services, including banking and insurance. Columbus is the headquarters for Nationwide and several smaller national insurance companies as well as being a major regional banking center. In the contexts of these two labor markets I undertook this study of young workers in their first "real" jobs. In the book's subsequent chapters I provide brief descriptions of the national and local labor markets for each of the sectors (e.g., industrial; financial, insurance, and real estate; and service) in which the young workers in this study located jobs.

FINDING WORK IN CINCINNATI AND COLUMBUS

Peter, one of the young workers who participated in the study, is a twenty-year-old appliance-repair worker employed in a relatively well-paying position repairing and overhauling air conditioners at $4.25 an hour. Peter was working in a small establishment in downtown Cincinnati at the time of his conversation with the interviewer in the summer of 1983.

The lengthy excerpt from a work-site interview that follows captures many of the sentiments expressed by the twenty-five young workers included in the study. Peter's point of view typified that held by many of the young men in the study. He was alternately hopeful about his own capacities and interests and dismayed at the tenuous nature of life in the latter part of the twentieth century:

INTERVIEWER: If you could look at yourself maybe five years from now, what do you think you will be doing?

PETER: That's hard to say. To tell you the truth, I want to still be doing this. It's the only thing so far that I've really liked. I don't think I could be sitting behind a desk. I wouldn't want to, to tell you the truth. I have to keep busy, even if it would be construction, using my hands. I'd have to do that before I'd sit down. Anyway, I'd have to be much older.

INTERVIEWER: How about ten years from now?

PETER: I don't know. I'll take it one day at a time.

INTERVIEWER: And how old are you now?

PETER: Twenty. I'll take it one day at a time. A lot of people say I'm crazy for going that way, but that's the way I'm going to do it, because who knows if this world's going to be here in ten years, the way things are going now. I'm not trying to scare you. My mom and I get in these arguments the same way. She says, "Plan for your future." But the world might not be here in another year. This whole place might be gone. It's true the way they are going about things, you don't know what could happen. I'm living for today. A lot of people my age are the same way. I guess the world isn't as good as it was when you were younger. It's worse,

the way I hear it. I can't look ten years ahead
and say I wish I was doing this. Because ten
years from now, as long as I'm surviving and
not living on the streets somewhere and have
someplace to live, I'm going to be happy.

We found a "live for the moment" orientation to be widespread
among young male workers in our study. Three attitudes dominated Peter's thinking and that of his white male peers: first, working
with one's hands has more value than holding a desk job; second,
the world created by the current generation of adult leaders is
extremely precarious; and third, opportunity for young people in
Peter's generation is more limited than in earlier times. The first
viewpoint is probably linked to social class; however, the second
and third are cohort effects which spring from the experiences of
Peter and his peers. In general, the views expressed by Peter and
others like him were very pessimistic. Indeed, their appraisals were
realistic: the economic recession showed no promise of lifting in
the near future, homelessness was becoming increasingly evident,
and the promise of perestroika and glasnost that we enjoy in the
early 1990s was by no way apparent.

Peter, born at the end of the "baby boom" era, entered the
work force after graduating from high school in 1982. He had no
preparation in appliance-repair work. After holding a job delivering
party supplies around town and working in construction, he
obtained this position, his first real job, repairing air conditioners,
stoves, and refrigerators, largely because his brother worked as
parts manager in the shop. He came to the labor market at a time
when there was a relatively large teenage cohort competing for a
relatively small number of jobs. Thus Peter was extremely fortunate in securing a job that demanded a relatively high level of skill,
ensured a fair amount of autonomy, and paid above the minimum
wage. In contrast, attitudes seemed far more variable and less
homogeneous among the young women in the study. For some, as
we will see in the case of Cindy later in this chapter, having any
kind of job simply to gain independence from parents and family
was the highest priority.

Entering the labor market and becoming established, reliable,
capable, and stable workers is extremely difficult for all youths, no
matter what their generation or whether they left high school as
graduates or dropouts. Several factors contribute to these difficulties. First are the institutional constraints imposed by businesses

and by the schools. Second are individual factors related to youth, such as inexperience and naiveté. Third, as discussed in chapter 1, are factors related to adolescence itself; during this developmental period youths are sorting out their identities, including their occupational identities. We will discuss the first of these factors here. The second and third points will be illustrated in later chapters as we document the young workers' experiences.

Institutional Constraints

Among the institutional constraints found in business is the employers' practice of hiring primarily on the basis of the interview (Bishop 1986). A problem with interviews is that frequently they are set up through referrals from vocational-education specialists or through relatives and friends employed by the business organization in question. This arrangement works well for youths who obtain referrals. Many others, however, including urban-dwelling African-American youths and urban Appalachian youths, have no contacts in business firms and were enrolled in few vocational education courses while in school, so that job opportunities in some occupational areas are inaccessible. Many of these youths were enrolled in the general track while in high school.

Despite employers' expressed desire for certain skills and attitudes in their newly hired young employees, their way of making hiring decisions ensures that they rarely consider specific educational skills or achievements beyond the number of years of school completed and the applicant's area of specialization. The focus on the high school diploma as opposed to job-related skills and abilities derives largely from two factors. First, businesses are reluctant to administer tests or to use test results in making hiring decisions because legal constraints and pressures from equal opportunity commissions have made these tests impractical, even though they would give a more accurate profile of the youth's actual capabilities than does the interview. Second, schools are notoriously unresponsive to employers' requests for transcripts and other related materials even when applicants request that these items be forwarded to an employer (Bishop 1986).

As a result of the general unresponsiveness of schools, employers tend to use the high school diploma as both the minimum and the maximum requirement. This practice provides employers with a strong rationale for paying the minimum wage to most youths entering the labor market, regardless of their job and skills.

Having *any* job is considered better than having no job by many young workers as well as by many adult workers; youths, however, rarely regard work as inherently meaningful or intrinsically satisfying (Kalleberg and Loscocco 1983). When asked about their jobs, most youths, particularly most African-American young women, respond as Cindy did when an interviewer asked what she liked about her job as a waitress in a fast-food restaurant. "What do I like?" Long pause. "I don't know. It's not that I like or dislike it, you know. It's just a way of making money, providing security or something."Cindy's job prospects are limited both by her relatively poor performance in high school and by her own apparent lack of enthusiasm for any of the work she had encountered. The lack of enthusiasm is understandable in view of the job contexts with which she is familiar. Probably it is a realistic strategy to place her occupational identity on hold or at least to delay her work future while she concentrates on meeting car payments and saving money to move into her own apartment, but we must question the social justice of her situation. Cindy's circumscribed opportunities lead her to view her job simply as a vehicle for making money.

Institutional Opportunities

Institutional constraints, such as employers' practice of using the interview rather than the applicant's high school transcript as the major source of information, are much more prevalent than institutional opportunities in providing access to jobs in the youth labor market. Nonetheless, somewhat unusual, almost idiosyncratic, talent-matching procedures can occur when a job applicant displays remarkable skills and abilities that the organization can use to its benefit. Capitalizing on athletic skills has been one of the few avenues of opportunity open to African-American males in the United States. Consequently, developing abilities in team sports such as basketball and football is a strategy that brings social acceptability as well as the promise of material rewards.

Reggie, the youngest of eight children, had been raised by his father's mother. Reggie's father had died when Reggie was two. His "brothers" and "sisters," the oldest of whom was forty-two, were actually his aunts and uncles, but Reggie regarded them as siblings. During the time of the study he lived with a brother and his brother's wife, who had helped him find a job as a bank messenger. He held this position during the time of our research. In an interview, Reggie explained how he had found his current job:

INTERVIEWER: Are you from Columbus?

REGGIE: No, I grew up in Pataskala, Mississippi.

INTERVIEWER: When did you move to Columbus?

REGGIE: After I graduated I came to live with my sister. But now I live with my brother.

INTERVIEWER: Do you two share an apartment?

REGGIE: No, I live with my brother and sister-in-law.

INTERVIEWER: How did you find out about Midland Bank?

REGGIE: My sister-in-law helped me fill out the application. They called me to work as a temporary since January. I played on the Midland Bank football team, and this guy wanted me to be able to play with them this fall. I needed a permanent status in order to play, so this guy pulled the strings to get me the job. I was lucky that was the policy, because now you have to be a full-time bank employee to be on the football team.

In the marginal comments, the interviewer concluded, "This is a great example of how an individual's sports skill opened doors so he could get a job." Indeed, employers at Midland saw an opportunity to enhance the bank's prestige by hiring Reggie to play football and basketball for the bank's teams.

At the bank, Reggie drove a small van from the downtown office to agencies and institutions around town with which the bank did business. He also sorted mail and made deliveries within the bank itself. Reggie's job as a messenger gave him considerable autonomy, an unusual feature in jobs typically held by young workers.

In addition, being an athlete made Reggie valuable to the organization and also provided him with a protected status. Two incidents observed during the course of the study illustrate how athletes can gain immunity and can receive preferential treatment within the structure of an organization's system of rules and opportunities.

During one of the runs from Midland's downtown office to a suburban insurance agency, the observer recorded the following statements:

Reggie sings with the radio. Reggie drives 70 mph. He sees the observer write this and starts laughing. He tries to cover the speedometer. The observer laughs, tells him that everything she writes will be withheld from his employer. He tells the observer the speedometer is broken, that 65 is really 55. All laugh. The observer asks if he's gotten a ticket while driving the truck. He says, "Yeh, but not for speeding".

OBSERVER: For what?
REGGIE: For taking a left-hand turn illegally. He and Tony (a co-worker) laugh.

During the course of the study, Reggie received at least two tickets while making runs for the bank in the van. He handed the tickets over to his supervisor, and they were paid routinely by the bank.

A major difficulty faced by Reggie and his mailroom co-workers was coping with changes in rules and procedures regulating their work. Frequent shifts in mailroom policy occurred because three different supervisors were appointed during the ten-month period when Reggie was observed at the bank. Kevin, Reggie's third supervisor, was a more hard-nosed boss than the person he replaced. As a new supervisor, he was especially concerned with security and discipline. One afternoon, while leaving the bank to make deliveries, Reggie drove the van at 30 miles per hour over a speed bump, stepped on the gas, and swerved playfully to avoid hitting a co-worker before encountering Kevin. The supervisor later disciplined Reggie through Pam, Reggie's immediate supervisor at the bank.

Reggie walks into the bank. He dumps the mail into a large bin. Pam is standing at the meter machine metering mail. Pam says to Reggie, "I've got to talk to you." Reggie says, "Okay," and begins to walk down the hall to make his deliveries. Pam says, "Kevin saw you playing around with the truck." Reggie looks confused. Pam continues, "On your last run Kevin saw you playing around." Reggie replies, "I waved to him. . . . " Pam says, "He also saw you swerve and chase Jack." Reggie says, "Oh, that." Pam replies, "Well, Kevin wants me to warn you. He said you could be taken off this job or possibly taken off the entire bank job [i.e., fired] if he sees that again."

After this encounter with Pam, Reggie and Fred (another mailroom employee) became sullen and defensive, protesting to each other that they would not stay at the bank for long unless Kevin became less strict. Indeed, things grew worse before they got better. A set of rules was imposed on the messengers requiring them to sign in and sign out, to remove keys from their trucks when making a delivery, and to comport themselves as dignified representatives of the bank.

Considerable grumbling continued among the mailroom staff, especially between Reggie and Fred, until Kevin made several accommodating gestures. First, he paid the crew to attend a two-hour meeting at which he provided food and during which he spelled out in detail the rules he wished to enforce. In addition, Kevin recognized that Reggie, Fred, and other young black male employees in the mailroom constituted a subcultural group linked primarily by their memberships on the bank's athletic teams. Moreover, he recognized that the bank's organizational image was tied to its athletic teams' success. Kevin's two-hour meeting, for example, was scheduled deliberately at a time that would not conflict with the basketball team's practice. Finally, rather than communicating through Pam or with other co-workers, Kevin began to deal more directly with Reggie, expressing his concerns in face-to-face conversation.

As we have seen, Reggie's skills in sports, particularly in football, not only provided entrée to his position at the bank but also gave him some protection from negative repercussions of his behavior on the job. Reggie also saw his skills as a ticket to the college career he wished to pursue at Ohio State University. While in high school he had been an All-State running back for his team. Reggie believed that he might be able to join the Ohio State team as a walk-on, a plan he was determined to pursue the following year. In the meantime he continued to work on his skills; ultimately he enrolled in a course at Ohio State during the winter quarter .

Institutional opportunities including access to jobs that provided autonomy and some measure of immunity, such as Reggie's job at the bank, were observed only rarely in the study. The other notable examples were found at the large amusement park, King's Island, which was owned at the time of the study by a major Cincinnati-based entertainment corporation with national and international ties. Young workers who performed in spectacular live productions on stage in the park were recruited frequently by entertainment meccas in Las Vegas, for the Broadway stage, and by major cruise-line companies.

Institutional opportunities for young workers in the form of access to interesting and even glamorous work, combined with the possibility for advancement and for a measure of personal fame, appear to be limited to youths with extraordinary physical talents and skills. It is important, however, to recognize that these kinds of opportunities are relatively rare overall and are available only to a fortunate few young workers.

FROM SCHOOL TO WORK:
NEGOTIATING A JOB

In moving from school to work, youths have three major areas of concern to negotiate: finding a job, settling into a job, and in many cases leaving one job and taking another. The average length of time youths spend on a job is six months, so leaving a job is a situation that most young workers confront. As we noted earlier, we followed twenty-five young people in Columbus and Cincinnati into their first real jobs after high school; by the end of the year we had visited forty-six work sites. Youths change jobs, and they do so frequently. Therefore, leaving a job is something they often must learn to manage.

Women and minorities, including the African-American women and the white urban Appalachian youths in this study, are particularly disadvantaged in locating a job. Teenage girls often receive fewer opportunities than boys to explore and plan their future careers while still in school. Girls enrolled in vocational education programs usually are trained to perform in a narrow range of low-paying clerical occupations; as a result they are particularly limited in their knowledge of how to get a job (Valli 1986). Youths from low-income and poor families often avoid more challenging job opportunities located outside their neighborhoods because such jobs disrupt important social networks of exchange among kin and peers. Often they create cultural conflicts that inexperienced youths cannot resolve easily (Ogbu 1986).

An example of this experience is provided by Jack, an urban Appalachian youth. Even though his parents had worked for years in the chain stores of a large Cincinnati bakery, Jack was not prepared for the interactional style of his flamboyant female boss. He was employed at a store in the chain located not in his neighborhood, but on the other side of town:

All the bakers said I was the best there. It wasn't that I wasn't catching on, or that I had a lack of understanding of the work or anything like that. It's my boss. She was this lady who'd want a hug and a kiss every night, and I didn't figure I was going into a job like that. I couldn't complain to the manager or the owner and tell them this stuff. Besides, she'd been working there for years.

Jack quit his job after three weeks and suffered long bouts of unemployment thereafter.

Holding a job requires a mastery not only of the job-finding process, but also of the social relationships required to manage the process of settling into a job (Borman 1988; Penn 1986). The most effective strategy for finding a job is to use informal networks, particularly friends or family members. Unemployed adolescent job seekers, primarily because they have limited resources of this sort, rely most often on less effective formal methods such as submitting a résumé, registering with an employment agency, and searching the classified ads. Once young job seekers have found work, they must settle into the job by making some accommodation to the work setting in order to survive there. To do so they must learn the labor process and negotiate interactions with co-workers and supervisors. As in Jack's case, young workers usually master the first task but often fail to master the second.

Certain organizational climates, particularly at banks and at other large institutions where routine mental labor is carried out by young female entry-level workers, appear to be less benign for these workers than others. Here young female employees generally are placed on the periphery of the action, far from other office staff members. In these settings they have very limited opportunity to become involved in the culture of the workplace. One young African-American woman recalled that after two weeks at a major Cincinnati bank she still did not know where the restroom was, much less what the bank's policies were regulating absences from work and the like. As a part-time employee whose hours extended from 10:00 AM to 3:00 PM, she was not expected to have a break, even for lunch. This was only one dimension of the overall isolation from her co-workers that she experienced daily. The organization's cultural capital was reserved for older, more experienced workers whom the organization viewed as more stable.

In chapters 3, 4, and 5 I will analyze the work lives of youths in settings corresponding to the three major labor market sectors that employ youths in the United States: (1) manufacturing, (2) finance, insurance, and real estate, (3) service. This research is based on an eighteen-month study; in most cases the twenty-five adolescents in the study sought full-time employment after graduating from high

TABLE 2.1
The Young Workers

Name	Education					Family		Siblings		
	Birth Date	Race/Ethnicity	Average Grade	Graduation Date	Program of Study	Father's Occupation	Mother's Occupation	Sex	Age	Occupation
Andy	5/20/65	White	D	1983	General 9–10 Voc. ed. 11–12	Past: GM worker Present: disabled	Past: secretary Present: unemployed	M F M	20 22 19	Fast-food work Secretary Student
Betty	8/14/64	White	A	1982	College prep. 9, 10, 11 Performing arts	Barber	Homemaker	M M F	27 22 18	Deceased Student at OSU Student
Cal	1/02/65	White	C	1983	General 9–10 Voc. ed. 11–12	Past: electrician Present: disabled	Homemaker	F M M	 45 36	In Florida Mental illness Babysitter
Cindy	11/24/63	African-American	C	1982	General 9 Voc. ed. 10 Voc. ed. coop 12	Father absent	Sales clerk	F F	Older Older	Homemaker Homemaker
Debbie	7/25/64	White	A	1983	General College prep.	Accountant	Assists husband	M		Divinity school

Name	Birthdate	Race		Graduation	Program	Father	Mother	Sex	Age	Occupation
Jack	1/09/64	White	C	Dropped out, 11th grade	General 9–10	Truck driver	Bakery manager	M	21	Real estate agent (FL)
								F	23	Restaurant worker
								M	Older	Construction worker
Miriam	3/05/62	African-American	B	1982	General 9–10 Voc. ed. 11–12	Foreman in Construction	Toy assembler	M	Older	Construction worker
								F	Older	School office worker
								M	30	Parts manager
Peter	3/17/63	White	C	1982	General	Construction worker	Homemaker	M	27	Construction worker
								M	25	Construction worker
Rod	3/02/65	White	C	Dropped out, 11th grade	General	Self-employed upholsterer and real estate developer	Bookkeeper	F	Older	Homemaker
								M	16	Student
Reggie	12/10/64	African-American	C	1981	College prep.	Died when Reggie was 2	Raised by aunt	M	16	Student
Val	3/10/65	White	B	1983	General 0–10 Voc. ed. 11–12	Pharmaceutical salesman	Company president	M	Older	Salesman
								M	Younger	Student

school, though a few had left school before graduating. All had finished their high school careers in 1980, 1981, 1982, or 1983 and had
obtained jobs in the Columbus or Cincinnati metropolitan areas.
Participants in the research were selected on the basis of (1) the labor
market sector in which their jobs were located, (2) individual characteristics including age, gender, level of education, and immediate
job-holding aspirations, and (3) their employers' willingness to allow
young workers to participate in the study.

As shown in table 2.1, the participants included approximately
equal numbers of young men and young women. With few exceptions these youths had grown up in lower-middle-class and working-
class homes, had achieved average grades, and had graduated or left
comprehensive public high schools, where they had been enrolled in
the general track or the vocational program. Most sought work
directly after leaving school and relied on relatives, friends, and
teachers for job-related information. Those who found jobs in this
manner stayed on the job longer than those who had relied on "help
wanted" ads in the paper or on other, similar sources.

Chapter 3 focuses on jobs in the manufacturing sector, specifically in a fastener factory and a sheet metal shop. Although these
industrial settings were common work sites for youths as recently
as twenty years ago, they have receded in their significance to the
youth labor market as manufacturing has slipped in its importance
to the overall economy. In chapters 4 and 5, I discuss young men and
women who hold jobs in the financial, insurance, real estate, and
new service-industry sectors. In each case study reported here, all of
the major areas to be examined—task technology, the reward system, and patterns of authority—depend on how the young workers,
co-workers, and supervisors negotiate the job—in other words, how
the young workers learn work tasks and carry out their work roles.
Thus the cases examined in this book continue the recent research
emphasis on the work setting as a negotiating arena (Burawoy 1979).

In order to understand how youths negotiate their jobs, we
must understand the labor process as a whole. As I have suggested,
this process depends heavily on four dimensions of the organization
of work in virtually all types of work settings. These dimensions are
(1) job task technology—how job tasks are organized and carried out;
(2) patterns of authority—the line of command from the supervisor
or manager to the worker; (3) the reward system—how work is rec-
ompensed; and (4) social interaction—how work lives are negotiated.

Two major informative models frame the analysis of these
aspects of the organization of work. The first, outlined in figure 2.1,

FIGURE 2.1
Causes of Worker Behavior

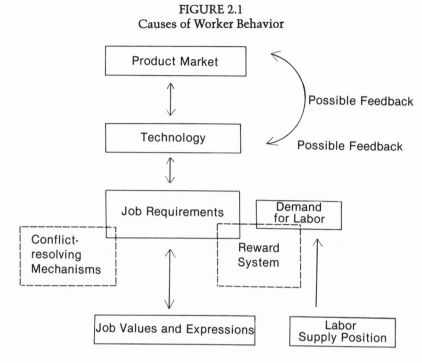

Source: Lupton, p.186

shows the relationship between the individual worker and the technological and economic factors influencing job requirements, values, and expressions. This conceptualizatîon is both macrosys-
temic and somewhat mechanistic. Although the influence of the
product market, job technology, demand for labor, and the like may
be more interactive and more irrational than this representation
allows, as suggested by segmented labor market theory, it is important to note that workers and work groups do not exist in isolation
from other forces outside the workplace. Bronfenbrenner (1979)
urges the analysis of individual socialization in the context of mul-
tiple systems of influence. Further, Charner and Fraser (1987), Mortimer and her colleagues (1979, 1986, 1990), and others argue cor-
rectly that generalizations surrounding the transition from school
to work for youths have been based on research studies that take a
narrow econometric view of the process rather than emphasizing
the influence of various institutional and environmental contexts
and the significance of social interaction.

TABLE 2.2
Classification of Manifestations of Autonomy

From the Worker's Point of View

	Overt	Covert
Individual	E.g., any observable, individual, secondary adjustments	E. g., daydreaming
Collective	Horseplay, singing, etc.	The "fiddle" (Lupton 1963); "banana time" (Roy, 1961–62)

From the Manager's Point of View

	Legitimate	Illegitimate
Tolerated	Behavior that is not against any rules and is not subject to any sanction	Mocking bureaucracy (Gouldner 1954), indulgency patterns, etc.
Not tolerated	Behavior that is not against any rules, but is subject to sanction, e.g., by foreman (manifestation of foreman's autonomy)	"True" defiance

The second analytic framework guiding the discussion in this and the following chapters is keyed closely to social interaction on the shop floor, in the bank, or in any other job setting. The variables outlined in table 2.2 support this framework. Because this conceptualization does not indicate paths of influence or causality, it is represented here as a typology of autonomy as manifested in various forms of workplace behavior, according to the worker's or the manager's point of view. Specifically, when work roles, job tasks, and other claims in which both workers and managers have a stake are to be negotiated, individuals may have to depend on rules that are neither evident nor binding (Morgan 1975). The distinction between legitimate and illegitimate behavior (from the manager's side) and between overt and covert behavior (from the worker's side) is important in any analysis focusing on the extent to which workers function either autonomously or in a manner highly dependent on workplace norms. Younger, less well-integrated workers (from management's perspective) are more likely to regard covert behaviors as the only route around management simply because they may lack the sophistication and experience of older co-workers (Borman and Hopkins 1987). We will see examples of such behaviors in chapter 3.

3. "YOU BUST ASS ON THIS JOB": WORK IN THE LIVES OF YOUNG FACTORY AND SHOP WORKERS

THIS CHAPTER EXAMINES THE work lives of two youths who hold traditional industrial jobs in plants: Jamie, a materials handler in a medium-sized factory, and Andy, a cutter in a small sheet metal shop. Before turning to these cases, however, let us examine the current context of the American manufacturing industry, which has changed dramatically over the past two decades. A major argument put forward in this book is that the cultural reproductionist view of the relationship between school and work is flawed, partly because it draws on the assumption that the modal or normative occupation for young workers in the United States and Great Britain is a factory job. As we will see, however, jobs in manufacturing sectors for all workers have declined precipitously over the last ten to fifteen years. There is little indication that the manufacturing industry will be a major source of employment in the near future (Noyelle and Stanback 1982). Furthermore, the cultural reproductionist view is limited because of its failure to consider either the collateral influence of other institutions, such as the family, or the impact of individual factors, such as the exigencies of youth as a period in the life course, on the ongoing social reproduction of individual lives.

Cincinnati, once the center of a vigorous machine tool industry, provides an example of the decrease in jobs in industrial manufacturing jobs. In July 1979, the last period of relatively full employment, the greatest number of jobs (174,500) in the Cincinnati area was found in manufacturing, compared to 120,700 jobs in the service sector. By July 1987, jobs in manufacturing had fallen to a total of 149,300; at the same time, service sector jobs numbered 169,500, making the service sector the source of the largest number of jobs overall (Cincinnati Enquirer, September 27, 1987). This pattern is characteristic of the nation as a whole; and it exemplifies employment trends in these two sectors during this period.

Although jobs in the manufacturing sector are no longer as plentiful as they once were, most prominent recent research studies of the workplace focus on industrial settings. Thus much of what we know about day-to-day experience in job settings prolongs the cultural reproductionists' "Marxist hangover" by preventing us from acquiring other images of work and job settings.

As pointed out in chapter 2, sociological studies of the workplace do not only investigate the extent to which young workers' characteristics mesh with employers' needs to provide institutional constraints and opportunities. They also emphasize the impact of the organizational milieu on young workers through socialization experiences. These latter investigations underscore the important role played by patterns of authority, the reward system, job task technology, and social interaction in the work group. Lupton (1976), for example, differentiates sociological analyses of workers' behavior from other research, including studies based on industrial engineering, economics, psychology, and human relations; he notes that sociological studies "describe and analyze in close detail the behavior of workers, usually of work groups" (192). An emphasis on the work group can be traced to the Hawthorne human relations research carried out in the 1930s. These studies documented the importance of moving beyond the "individualistic point of view" to understand issues in the industrial workplace.

In subsequent decades William Whyte was among the researchers who stated most forcefully that conflict between workers and management could not be resolved by changing workers' individual traits or characteristics. Instead, resolution would occur through understanding the impact of the social organization of the workplace on the worker and the way in which workers related to their place in the shop floor social system. In addition, Whyte argued that a focus on traits as they might be related to productivity was fruitless because "productivity seemed to fluctuate most directly . . . [in response to] changes in social activity and human relations" (Holtzberg and Giovanni 1981, 320).

Thus the Hawthorne research spawned a number of case studies in industrial settings, aimed at describing and analyzing in close detail various features of specific industrial organizations. These features included not only relations among workers but also the effects of status hierarchies, union–management relations, work flow, and informal organizations and voluntary associations on factory employees' productivity and work lives.

In the most recent research, factory settings are viewed as negotiating arenas. This focus can be seen as a continuation of that in the Hawthorne plant studies because it emphasizes the association between productivity and "social activity" among workers on the shop floor. A vivid illustration of this approach is Michael Burawoy's observational study, mentioned briefly at the end of chapter 2. Burawoy gained his initial experience as a participant observer employed as a machine operator in a Chicago-area die-cutting factory. His central concern was to explain the game of "making out," workers' efforts to achieve levels of productivity surpassing the 100 percent requirement in order to earn incentive pay (Burawoy 1979). The ceiling on making out established throughout the shop was 140 percent. This figure represented the formal agreement between labor and management, but in particular it reflected management's concern that turning out more work resulted in rate increases or "price cuts." Subsequently Burawoy discovered that workers systematically turned out more than this amount by devising strategies to reserve or invest "surplus" manufactured goods.

In order to maintain the system of making out, workers needed to establish relationships with co-workers and with their immediate supervisors, the shop foremen. Foremen granted "double red cards" when machinery in the shop failed or when materials were temporarily unavailable to production workers. These cards covered the time lost by workers through failures and delays at a rate of 125 percent. A great deal of negotiation accompanied signing a red card; the process involved such bargaining chips as permission to go home early, to attend union meetings, or to have "casual days" in return for better than 100 percent effort when the work crew was faced with a "hot job." According to Burawoy's observations, before the foreman signed the red card, "the operator had to persuade the foreman that he had made an earnest attempt to make out and therefore deserved compensation" (Burawoy 1979). The intriguing aspect to these negotiations is that "rules promulgated by high levels of plant management are circumvented, ignored, or subverted on the shop floor with the tacit and sometimes active support of the foreman, in the interests of making out" (Burawoy 1979). In other words, patterns of authority are *not* determined hierarchically, with dictates from the top enforced directly by those in the middle upon those below.

Although initially Burawoy was contemptuous of the game of making out because "it appeared to advance . . . [the company's] profit margins more than the operator's interests," he ultimately found himself "spontaneously cooperating" with management in the production of greater surplus value. He did so not because he experienced an awakening to a new value system congruent with management's stress on productivity, but rather because the social relations of the shop floor depended heavily on one's status in the process of making out (Burawoy 1979). In order not to be viewed as a troublemaker or as in league with the bosses and subsequently to be ostracized from the work group, it was important to become a dependable, cooperative participant in making out. Thus the labor process itself, rather than the attitudes and patterns of behavior that workers brought into the shop, guided interaction and behavior patterns in the factory. The organization of work was constructed through the dependencies developed among shop floor workers in their efforts to manipulate the reward system to their advantage. Young workers must become cooperative and reliable mates with their co-workers in factory and shop settings, but often their inexperience and naivete prevent them from having much influence on the floor.

JAMIE: FROM SCHOOL TO
    WORK IN THE FASTENER FACTORY

When Jamie was offered at age eighteen a job at Cincinnati-based Selco, the world's largest manufacturer of industrial staples, he became the youngest worker on the site. The Selco factory employed approximately 600 workers across three shifts to produce, pack, load, lift, and move boxes of staples from the production line to the warehouse and loading dock. Jamie found his job as a materials handler with little effort; approximately 70 percent of Selco's line employees, including his mother, were residents of Atlas, Jamie's hometown. His employment at Selco seemed almost inevitable.

Jamie never saw himself in the "brain part of it" while attending high school, but he hardly viewed his school career as a failure. Jamie had achieved recognition in his small, semirural community as a star on his high school's baseball team, playing third base, pitching as a reliever, and batting .429. At age thirteen he had placed third in the Cincinnati Reds batting contest. Nonetheless, the glamour of major league baseball had never attracted him seriously. During the interview reported below Jamie remarked, "If I went to college I would have probably played, I reckon. Other than that I wasn't thinking about becoming a million-dollar major league baseball player." Less than nine months after arriving at Selco, however, Jamie made the company team, while his co-workers did not. Although hardly comparable to becoming a million-dollar bonus baby in the major leagues, making the company team was an important indicator of high status among Jamie's co-workers.

Moreover, Jamie considered it important to be accepted and well liked by his co-workers, and he focused on fitting into his community's norms and values. In his case, in contrast to a middle-class standard, fitting in meant having "reduced aspirations" for mobility and working hard at jobs demanding heavy physical labor, such as lifting fifty-four-pound boxes of staples or planting, stripping, and racking tobacco on his stepfather's farm.

Like many of the young men and women who leave school for work, Jamie viewed becoming a materials handler at Selco as the result of a combination of factors: the lack of post-secondary education as an option, the physical proximity of the job, and recruitment by local townsfolk, including his mother, who had been employed at Selco for more than a decade when he was hired.

INTERVIEWER:	When you were in high school, did you have a notion about what you wanted to do when you finished?
JAMIE:	I didn't know what I was going to do when I got out; I had no idea. I kept hearing on the radio that there weren't no jobs. That gets you depressed. It surprised me that I got a job that quick. Really, I guess if it wasn't for my mom and all those guys down at the personnel office, I wouldn't have got a job down here, more than likely....
INTERVIEWER:	How were your grades in school?
JAMIE:	I was right around average.... Tanya Timm, she was a brain. She graduated with a 9.8. She's the one I cheated off of ... (grinning). No, she wouldn't let you cheat off of her. She

	figured she knew and wasn't going to let nobody else...[find out].
INTERVIEWER:	What did she end up doing?
JAMIE:	She went to Harvard....
INTERVIEWER:	How would you have felt about going to Harvard?
JAMIE:	I couldn't have went to Harvard. I was just never in the brain part of it.

The cultural capital that Jamie acquired in his family, school, and community emphasized the importance of physically demanding work in the factory, in the tobacco fields, and on the high school baseball team. Tanya Timm, the classmate who went to Harvard, was an exception to community and school norms in Atlas. Despite her working-class background, she acquired the elite cultural capital necessary to gain acceptance at a highly prestigious university. Because Tanya was not a participant in this study, it is not clear what factors were at play. The important point is that Jamie's cultural capital did not emphasize the "brain part of it." As far as he was concerned, Harvard was never accessible to him.

Job Task Technology

On a good night Jamie loaded six hundred boxes of staples during eight "runs" during his 3:30–11:30 P.M. shift. On each of these runs, he dropped off empty boxes and collected loaded boxes from the packers who were stationed at machines along the three aisles in the factory that were Jamie's territory. The task followed the same unvarying routine: two runs before the first break; two runs before lunch; two runs before the second break, and two runs before quitting time.

Two of the packers on aisle A/B enlivened Jamie's work routine, commenting unhesitatingly on his ability to do the job. Most often, however, they remarked on his status as the youngest worker in the factory, his inexperience, and his youth. Beneath the banter was a deep respect for the physical strength required to do the job. Patti, a co-worker, said to me, "He's a good boy. He works hard—you really bust ass on his job." The heaviest box of staples that Jamie slung from the dolly to the pallet and from the pallet to the forklift weighed fifty-four pounds.

Patterns of Authority

As we observed in the discussion of the subcultural perspective in chapter 1, lower-level workers in industrial settings and in other contexts where hierarchy appears to be clear are assumed to have less autonomy than either their managers or professional workers in other settings. In actuality, however, because they are engaged in a goods-producing enterprise, factory and shop workers have more tangible bargaining chips than workers who "produce" services. For the most part service work results in highly intangible outcomes; thus the workers have little leverage in negotiations with management. This situation, as we will see in chapter 5, may explain why clerical workers have not become unionized as readily as those whose work produces goods such as staples or dies. Although rates of production in manufacturing are established by management, they are negotiated in fact by workers and by their foreman on the floor as in Burawoy's die-cutting shop.

The principle of "discretionary insubordination" helps to explain what is negotiable, when it can be negotiated, and who is eligible to participate in negotiations. Young employees must establish their credibility as productive, reasonable, dependable workers before they can negotiate infringements of workplace rules (Corwin 1986). In both the fastener factory and the sheet metal shop (to be described later in this chapter), young workers were well aware of the existing patterns of authority in their workplaces, but they appeared extremely uneasy and confused about negotiating rules governing absences from work and leaving work or going on break early.

After they had been employed at Selco for approximately three weeks, Bill and Dan, two of the other four materials handlers who worked with Jamie, relied on a slightly older and more experienced co-worker rather than bargaining with their foreman to leave the shop floor a few minutes early. They wanted to use the company showers before picking up their dates and going out for the evening. Vic, an older member of the work crew, agreed to punch them out at 11:30. Because Vic was more familiar with the authority system of the workplace, he was incredulous at his younger co-workers' nervousness and fear of asking the foreman for permission to leave. Vic's reaction was reasonable because both his age and the greater length of time he had logged on the job made it appropriate for him to bend the rules if he chose to do so. In addition, Taylor, the foreman, was lax about enforcing strict adherence to a policy regulating hours on the floor. In fact, he appeared to tolerate activities that a naive observer might find disruptive and dangerous in a factory (Borman 1988). The following episode and the observer's comments illustrate Taylor's style:

At the end of the A/B aisle, a male packer teases Jamie about his method of picking up . . . [the boxes of staples]. The foreman approaches the observer and talks about his view of how to manage his area of production: "I'm on the floor 95 percent of the time. I know all of my thirty-seven employees by name. I know their employee numbers and dates of seniority." In addition, he . . . [states that he] stresses cooperation among the materials handlers and meets with them regularly to discuss the advantages of helping each other out.

Although Taylor generally exhibited a nonthreatening air, he was perceived as a grim authority figure by the younger, less experienced materials handlers. They saw his earlier experience in the Navy as a sure sign that he must possess an authoritarian personality. The materials handlers often finished their final prebreak run a few minutes before the appointed time. During these transitions, it was possible to observe their immediate response to the factory's regimen of authority as embodied in Taylor's presence on the factory floor.

All of the materials handlers have completed stapling the boxes from the last round. It is now dead time while they wait for the ten-minute break to begin at 5:30. Everyone is gathered around the materials station closest to Taylor's office in order to watch or assist in the operation of replacing the wheels on . . . a dolly. The cart is upside-down on the floor, and parts of the wheels are on the floor beside them. I ask how long the wheels last. Dan says, "I don't really know—they're used by all three shifts —so probably about three months."

They discuss the upcoming break. Taylor had a meeting with all of them last week to discuss new rules and regulations. No one is supposed to leave early for a break. Jamie says the rules don't go into effect until the twenty-fifth of the month. Vic says they have always been in effect but no one enforced them. Everyone watches the clock and Taylor's office.

JAMIE: Where is Taylor?

DAN: I don't know, but if we can't see him, he can't see us. (Jamie throws loose staples at Vic. Someone sees Taylor on the far side of the factory.)

VIC: C'mon. It's 5:25. He won't get back to see us until 5:30.

Immediately after this episode, the materials handlers left two minutes early for their ten minutes in the break room. They were convinced that Taylor was watching the clock, but were willing to engage in flaunting the rules because it was likely that they could get away with it (as they did).

The Reward System

Incentives at the nonunionized Selco factory were built into a system of immediate monetary rewards, generous benefits, and the long-term prospect of jobs in the factory's internal labor market. Institutional constraints existed in the form of limits on the array of jobs for those holding only a high school diploma, but institutional opportunities included paid tuition at any metropolitan college or university of the worker's choice.

Jamie's initial evaluation was made after his first ninety days. Taylor, his immediate supervisor, gave him a favorable performance review and increased his hourly wages. Jamie was fairly pleased; but he was not excited, because it was his perception that all the materials handlers received more or less the same review: "I think they do them in carbon copies."

During breaks, the subject of rewards emerged in discussions of salary schedules, company benefits, and positions available at Selco. Among the jobs on the factory floor, the position of materials handler was perceived by everyone as the most physically demanding and the least secure in the plant. Although the company was doing well, materials handlers, usually the most recently hired, were the first to be let go in hard times. Packers and even mechanics took over these positions when a low market demand for industrial staples led to layoffs.

Selco had a rather clear-cut classification system for hourly and salaried jobs. The company offered a generous benefits package; however, the materials handlers frequently demonstrated confusion, uncertainty, or lack of understanding both about the nature of these opportunities and about the most suitable method of pursuing them.

> During our break, we discuss salary schedules and the advantages of certain jobs in the factory. Jobs are either "prebid" or bid on after posting. Jobs rated "E" or lower are prebid. Only one of the materials handlers has an "E" designation. Tom points out that some hourly employees make more money than salaried workers. "J"-rated electricians are an example. Jamie scoffs, "You mean they make more than a foreman?" Tom replies, "No—but more than a clerical worker!"

Although the materials handlers understood that hourly and regular employees had different statuses in the factory, their knowledge of the factory's internal labor market was generally limited. They were aware that certain jobs were posted and others were not, and that eligibility for those positions was determined by such criteria as length of service to the organization and particular skills and abilities. Yet they had less precise knowledge about the salary structure, the corresponding occupational structure of jobs in the plant, and the internal labor market picture as it applied to their own mobility in the firm.

Jamie was not sure what he wanted to do over the next few years. A number of contingencies were affecting his choice of options, including pending decisions to marry and to leave tobacco farming. He expressed his ambivalence toward his present job and toward the contingent incentives and rewards as follows:

INTERVIEWER: What will you be doing five years from now?

JAMIE: I didn't know what I'd be doing when I got out of high school. I don't know. I don't have any idea. Hopefully, not picking up these boxes, that's for sure. Seems like a long time.

INTERVIEWER: If someone new were coming in to do the same job you're doing right now, what kind of advice would you give that person?

JAMIE: (Laughing) Ask for a transfer. (Becoming serious) I don't know. It's your own pattern in there—it is however you want to do it. Ain't no one of us in here does the same thing, the way we put out boxes. We start at the same thing . . . [as materials handlers] but that's about it. You just got to do whatever feels comfortable to you. . . .

INTERVIEWER: What would you say are the best parts about this job?

JAMIE: Money. It's a lot better than anybody's making up there that I graduated with. It still ain't my lifelong dream.

INTERVIEWER: What would you say are the worst parts of it?

JAMIE: Punching a time clock. I was used to farming. You'd go out there when it was cool and quit when it got hot. . . . One thing, I got a little saved up, especially if I get laid off or something. And no job security. One day I'll get married, I reckon. That's a long ways down the road, too, I think. Dean . . . [a co-worker] keeps telling me to put my money in an IRA. He says social security ain't going to be worth a dime. I don't know. I might start doing that. I will be a millionaire by the time I'm sixty-five (laughs). . . . (Becoming serious) I don't know what I'm going to do . . . [to become] a millionaire!

Another reason for Jamie's uncertainty about his future at Selco stemmed from his perception of the decline in factory work and the rise of technology in the plant: "Factories ain't going to be around a whole lot longer, are they? As far as people working there. They keep building these autopacks and all that kind of stuff." Although technology did not immediately threaten Jamie's position, it was present as an impending long-term problem in its potential for disrupting employment patterns at Selco. As we will see in chapter 4, technology has already turned employment in clerical jobs topsy-turvy.

ANDY: FROM SCHOOL TO WORK IN THE SHEET METAL SHOP

Much like Willis's lads, Andy and his friends "bombed out" during their senior year in a Columbus-area high school by being rowdy in class and by cutting classes altogether when they could. During his last year in the vocational program, Andy spent most of his time avoiding his teachers and his classes, which were conducted in the high school's Career Center. Andy and his interviewer had the following exchange regarding one teacher's reaction to Andy and his friends during this period:

ANDY: It was a boring class, but we was kind of rowdy. He used to get upset with us. We used to come in drunk and stuff. He used to get mad.

INTERVIEWER: Can you understand why?

ANDY: (Misunderstanding the interviewer's question) It was boring.

INTERVIEWER: The class was boring? How do you feel about classwork compared to what you do at Square D?

ANDY: At the Career Center, we laid a lot of stuff out; at Square D, we don't hardly lay nothing out.

In moving from school to the shop floor, Andy changed from following a pattern of behavior that included getting drunk regularly in order to tolerate boring classes to working in a setting where there was more than enough to keep him busy; he valued this set of circumstances. Drinking still was a major social activity, but Andy attempted to confine it to weekends when he and three friends easily went through a couple of cases of beer.

Not all of Andy's friends made the transition from school to work as successfully as he did. Cal, who was hired at Square D in the spring of 1983 at the same time as Andy, lost his job after failing to produce accurate work at a pace that met the shop's demands. Cal's parents were completely exasperated by his behavior, which included heavy bouts of drinking with his friends followed by citations for driving under the influence of alcohol. These problems led to Cal's conviction on a charge of reckless driving and drivng under the influence (DUI), and eventually resulted in his three-day imprisonment. We will explore the implications of these two patterns—one adaptive, the other not—later in this chapter.

Task Technology

Although Andy was engaged in highly routinized work at the sheet metal shop, his success on the job eventually introduced some variation into the daily round. Andy's routine at Square D began at 8:00 A.M. and invariably followed the same pattern, no matter what specific job he was assigned by Lloyd, the foreman. This pattern is shown in the following set of three related episodes that occurred during three different shifts:

Episode 1. Andy picks up a set of directions from Lloyd's desk, goes to the machine shop, and begins to shear metal on the old shear.

Episode 2. Lloyd says, "Okay, now that you have that done ... " and gives him a new task. Andy goes into the second room and begins measuring scrap to find out which pieces he should use for his new assignment. Lloyd yells in to Andy to pull twenty-six sheets at five feet and to slit them at 27 1/2 inches. Andy nods to himself.

Episode 3. Andy arrives at the shop on time. He walks over to where Lloyd is working on the shear and receives his first assignment for the day. He is making "S-hooks." This task is accomplished by feeding sheared pieces of metal . . . perhaps 3" x 10" into the machine . . . they exit from the machine as finished components. This is definitely an easy task compared to what Andy usually does.

When Andy started a new job, he either obtained instructions from the supervisor's desk or received them directly from Lloyd. Then he gathered the appropriate sheet metal pieces or scraps and walked to the shears or to the slitter, machines used in trimming, cutting, and notching the metal. On some days Andy cut blanks; on others he fabricated plenums, metal boxes placed on top of furnaces.

By the time Andy had been at Square D for a year, the sheet metal shop manager had come to regard him as a highly valued specialist. During an interview with the manager, the researcher asked how Andy fit into the task structure of the shop.

> MANAGER: [Andy does] three or four tasks that no one else does. Plenums demand accuracy and flexibility. We make every one of those to special order . . . He'll take a look at . . . [the order], and by looking at the description he's able to go and manufacture the number of pieces at the proper size that will make a particular box. Each one is custom made. Right now, he's probably making fifteen or twenty of these a day—almost every one a different size.

All the pieces that Andy sheared were components of ductwork used in constructing heating systems. A major dimension of his work was monitoring his own production of these pieces, much as Jamie kept track of the boxes of staples he collected during a run. Whereas Jamie had a clipboard attached to his dolly, on which he recorded the evening's work, Andy counted the fabricated pieces in his head while he cut and sheared the metal.

During the hour in his shift described partially below, Andy completed an order for 350 collars and an order for S-hooks. Although the observer estimated that the production process was considerably faster than it actually was, her claim that Andy sheared one strip per second was based on the perception that his dexterity, speed, and control of the process enabled him to work at a rapid pace.

Andy walks over to Lloyd's desk and picks up some instructions. He walks to the shears and begins to cut 1" by 3" pieces and then cuts these into 1" x 1-1/2" strips. He takes all the metal in the scrap pile under the shears and throws out pieces that can't be cut into strips. He gets about fifteen pieces trimmed to size. He adjusts the machine to cut the 1" x 1-1/2" strips. He begins to cut these strips quickly—I'd estimate one per second once he gets the piece set into the shears. He tosses the scrap pieces onto a pile.

Lloyd comes over and makes a very fine adjustment in the shears. He says something to Andy. Andy does not respond. Lloyd checks Andy's pieces already cut. He says something to Andy and Andy says, "Yup." Andy has completed the first order.

Andy goes to the stack of sheet metal in the corner and picks up a fresh piece of metal. He cuts two pieces of different dimensions. He cuts off the corners. He brings these two pieces into the other room and binds the corners. He gets four more pieces of metal and cuts the corners and then binds two sides of these pieces with the electric bender. He goes to the hard bender to get the other two sides bent. He marks the stock and makes eye contact with me. I ask, "Was that an order?" He shrugs and says "I guess."

Andy goes back to sorting out the pieces of metal and trimming them to the right size to mark the 1" x 1-1/2" metal strips. He cuts about ten sheets into strips. I ask, "How do you keep track of how many you've cut?"

ANDY: You just count as you cut.
OBSERVER: You've been counting the whole time?
ANDY: Yeah.
OBSERVER: How many do you have?
ANDY: Eighty-five.
OBSERVER: How many do you need?
ANDY: Fifteen more.

In this setting, as well as in the bank and insurance settings that we observed, regulating one's task-related behavior by monitoring the production of metal strips or by tracking the number of canceled checks processed for a particular client appeared to be important in managing rather routine task technologies.

Patterns of Authority

At Square D most of the young workers were hired from the vocational program that Andy had attended. The person who did the hiring was Lloyd, who also trained and supervised these workers. Lloyd was a colorful figure; he spoke frequently of his "fits," caused by several unhappy marriages, chain-smoked on the job, and seemed to have a real empathy for his junior co-workers. Lloyd was ambivalent about recruiting young workers from the vocational program primarily because he thought they were overtrained for the work he assigned. One observer comments as follows:

> After Jane [another observer] and I break for lunch, we listen to Lloyd talk. He speaks of the boys' training . . . [in vocational school] versus the low-level tasks he has to make them do at the shop. "It's a waste; sometimes it works better to have a guy off of the street who doesn't know anything."
>
> Lloyd says that he prefers to hire right off the street than . . . [to hire] vocational graduates because there is not enough variety in the work to keep their interest. There has always been turnover in the shop. People move on to various kinds of jobs. One person left because of drugs—joints. Lloyd says that Cal is more interested in cars and women than in working. "Don't blame him," Lloyd comments. "You are not hiring experience. You are hiring $3.50 an hour. Not really that much room for advancement either. It's a shame to do this to kids from the vocational school. At least they get some experience."

As personnel man, supervisor, and trainer, Lloyd had considerable influence on the work flow in the shop. He also seemed to have an unusual understanding of the mesh between youths' skills and marketplace opportunities and constraints, as is clear in his previous statements. Tom Ellsworth, however, the manager of Square D, reviewed workers' job performances and made decisions about promoting or firing workers. Thus lines of authority went directly from Andy and his co-workers to Ellsworth.

One outcome of the previously described pattern of hiring procedures at Square D was the establishment of friendship groups on the shop floor. These tight cliques had the potential to erode workplace authority. One event that became legendary in the shop was "Andy's long lunch." It occurred on the first pleasant spring day, and involved Andy and two co-workers from the vocational school. The incident was explained by Ellsworth during an interview:

Three young men—Andy, a young man named Rick, and a young man who ... was coming in while he was in school, went out to lunch one day and they never came back. They called Don Harmony, the operations manager, who was out to lunch, and left a message that they had a flat tire. Well, they went out to have lunch, and evidently they had a flat tire and for some reason couldn't make it back. They go to lunch around noon, and we are open to 4:30 ... they went maybe two or three miles away, [and] all three of them came in the next day sunburned. There were some questions. ... How long does it take to change a flat tire? [Do] you always get sunburned when you have a flat tire? ... The young man named Rick, instead of just saying "I blew it," he continued to press the issue and ended up in a heated conversation with the operations manager. He was told, "If you don't like it you can leave," and he left. But Andy never got that far. I believe Andy said he was at fault for not coming back. It was the first nice day we had this spring in early May or the end of April. I would say it was a matter of the way Rick handled himself with Don Harmony. Most supervisors don't like people to talk back to them or to question their judgment, especially when they are completely in the wrong. It doesn't take four and a half hours to change a tire even if you have to go get one. The other people involved could have asked for a ride or something to get back. So Rick was let go. When I was running the sheet metal shop, one of the other students I know that was in the study, I let him go because of his job performance. But that was after having several long discussions with him and ... [allowing a] thirty-day probationary period. ... [These were] weekly discussions for a month, sitting down once a week saying, "Look here's your errors; you were given twenty ... [lists] to cut and ten of them have errors. We just can't live with that ... [I mean] from a job-performance standpoint." To be completely honest, to be fired at our company you really have to do something bad. That's just the way things run.

The employee whom Ellsworth fired after this incident was Cal, who had started at the shop at about the time Andy was hired. During extensive work-history and current-events interviews with the researchers, the phrases Cal used most frequently to describe his work-related activity were, somewhat ironically, *taking a break* and *getting a fresh start*. He was never able to do the latter during the ten months he remained in the study after leaving the sheet metal shop. During most of this period Cal was unemployed, jailed on a drunk-driving charge, laid up by a bad back, or incapacitated by other physical complaints. Because he still lived at home, Cal continued to be a source of unhappiness to his father. Many of his problems had surfaced during his stint at Square D and had led to his dismissal. Cal's fate was reported to one of the researchers:

> Tom Ellsworth telephoned...that Cal had been fired this morning. Cal had not worked the past two days, claiming that he hurt his knee on the break...[i.e., a machine] and that his leg had swelled up. He was also out...on Monday due to his court appearance...[on a DUI charge], missed one half day Friday because he overslept, and had made mistakes on the job Friday afternoon and Tuesday. Friday he didn't cut the metal right, and Tuesday he cut twelve pieces when he had been asked to cut eighteen pieces. He also told Ellsworth that he wouldn't be able to come to work Friday because he was supposed to return to the family doctor about his knee. However, he had also told the bookkeeper that he would pick up his check because he was planning to go out of town over the Fourth of July weekend.

Cal's family of origin was similar to Andy's, according to standard indicators of socioeconomic status, such as parents' level of education, occupation, and the like. Yet, although Cal's family was intact, his father was in ill health and unemployed. His mother appeared to want to protect him from a calamitous world; she referred to him as her baby, tiptoed around the house when he slept until midafternoon, and viewed his problems with drinking and the law with mildly glum resignation.

A period of floundering during late adolescence is considered normative by psychologists such as Erik Erikson, who argues that identity formation is the major developmental task facing youth. In the case of middle-class males, a moratorium in developing a strong occupational identity might be accommodated by attending college and either changing majors frequently or delaying commitment to a course of study for as long as possible. In the case of working-class youths, however, college often is not an option.

Andy lived at home with his parents and younger brother. His older brother had left home recently after a fight had erupted between himself and the father from whom the older boy had stolen a sum of money. Andy's leisure time appeared to be organized largely to avoid his family as much as possible. His girlfriend, a sophomore in high school, lived within walking distance of his home. Two or three times a week he trekked to her home after dinner to watch television with her and her mother. On weekends Andy and his girlfriend partied, shopped at the mall, and attended a rock concert when Blue Oyster Cult, Black Sabbath, or some other heavy-metal band was in town. Andy said the following about his use of marijuana as opposed to beer or hard liquor:

ANDY: I don't drink beer that often. I just got into the habit of smoking dope. But I don't do it before I go to work.

INTERVIEWER: Do you smoke with the guys you ride home with?

ANDY: No, with friends . . . with my girlfriend, she doesn't do it that often.

INTERVIEWER: How often a week would you say you smoke (dope)?

ANDY: About three or four days and over the weekend.

INTERVIEWER: So about three or four days during the week, two or three days on the weekend. You do this with friends in the neighborhood. . . . So this is where some of your money goes . . . into buying that? About how many ounces do you use a month?

ANDY: About one. My mom all the time tells me, "You ought to quit buying that stuff."

INTERVIEWER: Your mom knows?

ANDY: Yes.

INTERVIEWER: What else does she say?

ANDY: She quit. She used to get on my case.

INTERVIEWER: She used to smoke it?

ANDY: No, she don't do nothing.

Although Andy was focused on continuing his job as a sheet metal worker, a trade with which he identified strongly, he experienced difficulty in gaining independence from his family and moving on from the beer-drinking, dope-smoking, heavy-metal music-loving "guy" that he had been during high school.

Yet although Andy's transition from school to work was easier than Cal's, his personal development appeared to be far more painful. Andy suffered two losses during the period of the study, both of which hit him hard. The first was the loss of his car, which occurred as the result of an accident in which he was involved.

INTERVIEWER: When did this accident happen?

ANDY: A month ago. It was on a Friday or a Saturday night.

INTERVIEWER: What kind of car did you ruin?

ANDY: Maverick.

INTERVIEWER: Was it totaled?

ANDY: No, it wasn't totaled, kind of bent up the front bumper. That's the only thing that showed. You couldn't open the door, the driver's door. That's the only thing it really did to it. It ripped some wires below. Me and my brother-in-law fixed all of that, got it running, then a couple of weeks later it just...[died].

INTERVIEWER: So are you going to get another car then?

ANDY: Yeah.

INTERVIEWER: How much money do you have saved for it?

ANDY: Three hundred and fifty dollars. I'll need that by Friday to get this car I want, but I doubt it will happen. My mom won't sign for a loan. She won't give me no money.

INTERVIEWER: So you don't have the car. It's tough trying to find a car for $350, huh?

ANDY: It cost twelve hundred dollars but $350 down. It would take me over a month to get that much saved. I ain't got no spending money, and if I bought a car, between paying on the payments for my car, insurance, and the house, I'd have about teñ bucks left. I only make a hundred and twenty bucks a week. I spend all of that paying bills. It's tough.

INTERVIEWER: Yeah, it's tough. It doesn't leave much money for movies and dating or things like that.

Andy's second loss was the loss of his girlfriend who was four years younger than he was.

INTERVIEWER: Do you have a girlfriend?

ANDY: No.

INTERVIEWER: Do you see yourself getting married some-day? Not since you broke up with the ex?

ANDY: No.

INTERVIEWER: You don't want to get married?

ANDY: No, that's the last time I fall in love.
INTERVIEWER: How come?
ANDY: I ain't going through that shit no more.
INTERVIEWER: What happened?
ANDY: I was depressed hard, for about two weeks. Then I started realizing I don't need it.
INTERVIEWER: Did she break up with you?
ANDY: Yeah. We were fighting a lot.
INTERVIEWER: What were you fighting about?
ANDY: Stupid little things, just getting on each other's nerves. She acts like a little girl.
INTERVIEWER: But you're still good friends with her mom?
ANDY: Yeah. I go over and talk to her, drink a beer with her, smoke a joint. That's why I'm so cool with all of her relatives. They all party.
INTERVIEWER: All of her relatives party? Does she?
ANDY: I think I got her started. I think she's going to be a drug addict soon. She's going to die; she's a lude freak. I got her on ludes, and she just fell in love with it. I created a monster. She's been begging me for all kinds of drugs. I won't buy her nothing no more. I told her mom I wouldn't. It's over, and I won't give her nothing. She's going to have to go to her mom now.
INTERVIEWER: Well, yeah, that's what happens. I can't blame you.

It was difficult to tell which event, the loss of his Maverick or the separation from his girlfriend, had a greater impact on Andy's well-being. Among working-class males there may be a more finely differentiated set of expectations for masculine than for feminine behaviors. Although Andy might engage in such activities as drinking and smoking dope, it was reprehensible not only that his former girlfriend was soon to become a drug addict and might even die soon from her Quaalude habit, but also that Andy had indeed been responsible for "creating a monster."

In the growing men's studies literature, the problem of gender relations in the social construction of masculinity is an important issue. According to Kimmel (1988), "Masculinity . . . is a relational construct and is to be reconstructed, reasserted or redefined in relation to changing social and economic conditions and the changing position of women in society" (153). Many scholars, including Kimmel, see that increasing numbers of men are recognizing the ways in which their ability to transform masculinity is inspired and made possible by the women's movement. Such recognition, however, is difficult and painful. It is unlikely that young working-class males in our society will be moved easily or soon to seek alternative leisure pursuits, or that a vision of sexual equality or gender justice will inspire them to transform traditional masculine forms such as the "jock" or the "guy."

The Reward System

Andy's salary increases reflected an overall assessment of his job performance as well as other dimensions of his demeanor as a worker, including attitude, accuracy, overall competence, and relationships with other employees. The rational basis for this multidimensional review was embedded in the organization's management system, which I will consider shortly.

Work in the sheet metal shop was structured to include a range of tasks with varying demands; this feature of the shop's reward system was unique among work settings that employed young workers. In contrast to workers in the sheet metal shop, materials handlers in the fastener factory carried out their work in an unvarying routine of never-changing tasks. This is the usual pattern of jobs in the secondary labor market that young workers characteristically hold. Andy progressed through his first training period and the corresponding job responsibilities in the spring of 1983, when he was still in school and was working part time at Square D. When he began to work for the company full time that summer, his performance review was good enough to warrant a change in his job assignment. This change also told Andy that he was performing well and that his accuracy and speed were valued, particularly in comparison with other young workers from the same vocational education program. According to Ellsworth, the manager:

> He rose very rapidly to a position which you could consider higher than the fellow that was there before him. Because of the way he worked and his accuracy and his speed, he continually progressed and moved on to other things, whereas that other fellow . . . [from the same vocational program] who was there when he got there, was pretty much stuck in the position he was stuck in because he just couldn't cut the metal right and wouldn't cut the metal right.

Monetary rewards were not tied directly to performance evaluations, which were carried out every thirty days for new workers, although Andy's evaluation was linked to a salary increase. When the interviewer asked Ellsworth whether Andy had perceived this performance review as fair and accurate, he responded, "I think so. He left with a smile and a raise."

In addition to the regular evaluations, which were structured to review on-the-job behavior and performance, self-evaluations were carried out by employees after they had been with the organization for at least a year. This highly rational system of performance review and on-the-job evaluation, in addition to an enlightened employee bonus package and company ownership plan, was encouraged by the presence of Howard Samuels, chairman of the board at Square D and former president and owner of the company. Samuels had installed a trusted colleague as president when the demands of a second career interfered with his full investment in the day-to-day operations of the shop. Manager Ellsworth viewed the shop as "unique," and probably he was correct in this view of the shop's enlightened management:

> [Howard Samuels], the chairman of the board also has a doctorate in finance. He went back to school in the late sixties and got his doctor's degree somewhere around seventy-two or seventy-three, so he's spent probably the last ten years teaching. He doesn't spend at the most three or four hours a day at the office and probably . . . [comes in] no more than two or three days a week. He's a professor of finance at Capital University at their graduate school. He hasn't had a hand in the operation of the company for probably the last ten years; the president of the company has done it. Even though we're in transition . . . [to company ownership by employees through a shareholding arrangement], the person running the company . . . [as president] is the person that probably owns the majority of the stock at the present time. So there isn't really a conflict between who owns the company and who is running it. . . . When the transition was made, and Howard Samuels became chairman of the board and John Baldwin became president, Howard set guidelines and rules that were not covert, and there was no reason to go talk to Howard about anything from that point on. If you've got a problem, you work it out with John. That's the way it works.

As we have seen in the previous discussion of manufacturing jobs, there are intimate connections among organizational arrangements, labor market structures, and individual work experiences. Not only have jobs in the manufacturing sector declined; this erosion of jobs also has affected patterns of recruitment of youths into jobs and has influenced their subsequent training.

Employers in both the fastener factory and the sheet metal shop were likely to recruit young workers from familiar sources: the local small-town labor pool or a specific vocational school's program. Thus although gaining access to a factory or shop job is critical, careers in these two cases proceed with few roadblocks and considerable support from management once access is gained. Indeed, both settings appeared to the observers to be extremely supportive of the young workers in the study. Certainly it is likely that firms with fairly benign work atmospheres would be more likely to accommodate this research project, but not all work environments were in fact hospitable to their workers even while they welcomed us.

The cases considered in this chapter urge researchers to be cautious when describing manufacturing jobs as dehumanizing, hierarchical, and dominated by organizational constraints. The white males who typically hold these positions appear to have access to a number of obvious benefits, including better than average wages and at least in Jamie's case, an internal labor market characterized by opportunities for advancement. We can assume, then, that not all individuals employed in the manufacturing sector face hopeless, dead-end careers. In fact, it appears that goods-producing businesses value highly the individual contributions made by young employees who are productive (Zuboff, 1988). Finally, recent studies of shop floor settings, such as Burawoy's study of the die-making factory, have been useful in explaining how the industrial setting is not merely the locus of goods production. These studies, however, are limited by an exclusive focus on the industrial setting. It is critically important to gain an understanding of the social construction of young workers' identities as it occurs in overlapping institutional contexts, particularly work and family. In order to grasp this process as completely as possible, we also must gain access to the lives of people outside the work setting. In addition, we must explore settings other than the factory or the shop in order to understand the effects of the full range of youths' jobs.

4. "THEY DON'T LIKE YOU TO TALK HERE": WORK IN THE LIVES OF YOUNG CLERICAL WORKERS

FINANCIAL INSTITUTIONS IN Columbus and Cincinnati have long-standing records of hiring female clerical workers upon their graduation from local area high schools. Employers remarked that they preferred graduates from parochial schools, presumably because they were more docile and less likely to resist patriarchal authority. This chapter considers three cases: Betty, a clerical worker at Midland Bank in Columbus; Miriam, whose case is explored less fully, a clerical worker at River City Bank in Cincinnati; and Val, a clerical worker who was given the title of administrative marketing specialist soon after her employment, at Midwest Insurance in Columbus. None of these young women, it should be noted, had attended a parochial school.

In the realm of clerical work, the impact of technological change has been strongest among workers in telecommunications and microprocessing. The field of microprocessing as a whole and the clerical system that supports it are dominated by women whose working conditions and job opportunities are the principal subject of this chapter.

According to the National Research Council's Panel on Technology and Women's Employment (1986), technological developments in recent decades have led to sweeping changes in the organization of work, major sectoral employment shifts, and alterations in the pattern of women's work-force participation. Specifically, the reorganization of secretarial work into word processing tasks has occurred as a result of major technological advances in data entry, data storage, and processing, output, and display technologies. These developments have enabled clerical workers to key information into systems that allow rapid word entry and quick subsequent access to stored data.

On the positive side, as word processors give way to personal computers and work stations, more far-reaching effects may occur. The lines between secretarial and professional/managerial work may blur as secretaries increase their access to important data and their ability to manipulate this information so that they can generate analytic reports; the locations of work may become more flexible with the advent of stand-alone equipment and telephone access to centralized data bases; and a reduced need for paper record keeping may alter work organization even more dramatically (National Research Council 1986, 11). Yet, although this scenario emphasizes increased power, autonomy, and job enhancement for secretarial workers, technological change also has a less positive side. First, even though centralization of information may provide greater access to information for on-line users, it also may be used as a device by management to keep clerical workers on their toes, as is shown dramatically in the case of Betty at Midland Bank. Advances in telecommunications have allowed major banking and insurance companies to monitor employees' productivity, as measured by the volume of calls taken each day, their "friendliness" toward customers, as determined by their tone of voice, and their ability to handle incoming calls, as shown by the number of pauses in conversations with clients. Such advances have increased the remoteness of management and the alienation of workers in many large, bureaucratic financial settings (Zuboff 1988).

Second, in addition to altering the organization of work, technological change also has altered employment patterns across labor market sectors. As shown in table 4.1, women's employment in white-collar jobs has surpassed their employment in both blue-collar and farm jobs increasingly since the 1950s. In 1980, clerical jobs employed almost twice as many women as the next-largest occupational subgroup, "other services," which claimed 18.8 percent of the female labor force. In addition, women are concentrated in a relatively small number of occupations, according to the National Research Council, "because they are sometimes less geographically mobile, and because their access to education, training, or promo-

TABLE 4.1
Major Occupational Groups of Employed Women, 1950–80 (Percentages)

Occupation	1950	1960	1970	1980
Total women	100.0	100.0	100.0	100.0
White-collar workers	52.5	56.3	61.3	63.5
Professional	12.2	13.3	15.5	15.9
Managers	4.3	3.8	3.6	6.8
Clerical	27.4	30.0	34.8	33.8
Sales	8.6	8.3	7.4	7.0
Blue-collar workers	43.9	41.8	37.9	35.5
Crafts	1.5	1.3	1.8	1.8
Operatives	20.0	17.2	14.9	10.7
Laborers	0.9	0.7	1.0	1.3
Private household	8.9	8.3	3.9	3.0
Other services	12.6	14.4	16.3	18.8
Farm workers	3.6	1.9	0.8	1.0
Managers	0.7	0.6	0.2	0.3
Laborers	2.9	1.3	0.6	0.7

Source: Bianchi and Spain 1984, Table 3 (National Research Council 1986)

tion within and across firms may be more limited than men's" (National Research Council 1986, 19). In other words, women not only suffer *institutional* constraints, such as limited or no access to internal labor markets, but also are hindered in their career aspirations as a result of negative effects of widespread *societal* discriminatory practices. It is expected, for example, that women will put aside their own career ambitions in deference to their husbands' plans.

The National Research Council panel appears to be rather tentative in holding organizations and labor markets accountable for the lack of employment and job advancement opportunities for women as well as for women's relatively disadvantaged status across market sectors. Other observers, however, have been less reserved in their negative appraisals of the causes and consequences of sectoral employment shifts and of the patterns of women's workforce participation. Baron and Bielby (1985), for example, in investigating the relationship between organizational arrangements and career outcomes for workers in fifty California firms, determined that internal labor market dynamics discriminated systematically against women and in favor of men. In one manufacturing plant the researchers noted that disparities in opportunities for advancement were inherent in job classifications and in "tilted" sex ratios among job incumbents. Although "assemblers" (women) and "production workers" (men) performed the same duties, these jobs were "conspicuously different in relation to organizational promotion hierarchies.... Workers were segregated by sex upon entry and then channeled into sex specific career trajectories" (Baron and Bielby 1985, 242). Women in the manufacturing plant were far less likely to become supervisors than their male counterparts, because the ratio of female supervisors to line workers placed women at a distinct disadvantage. Whereas a leadlady typically supervised fifty-five employees, a leadman was in charge of eight workers, a mere handful by comparison. This lopsided arrangement led directly to far more favorable advancement opportunities for male supervisors.

In office settings, clerical work no longer provides access to promotions to other positions within firms, as it once did. Office workers' jobs and their opportunities for salary increases and prestige enhancement vary according to the worker's status: she may be a private secretary assigned to a boss, or a member of a typing pool, a role that is likely to provide few opportunities to achieve recognition. Recognition is important in large, bureaucratic office settings, as Kanter (1977) has shown. Occupational advancement for secretaries in large firms is contingent on their bosses' promotions and advancement, although this has not always been the case. At the turn of the century, as the typewriter mechanized clerical work, females were recruited to hold the positions in large firms that formerly had been occupied by males. Men previously had been promoted to supervisory jobs from these positions, but now they deserted the clerical ranks to seek entry-level positions that provide more autonomy. According to Lowe (1987):

> By the 1930's, women formed a new subordinate class of clerical functionaries, relegated to the most routinized and mechanized tasks—a trend that still persists today (199).

In addition, Lowe contends that in contrast to Braverman's (1974) characterization of the office as a factorylike setting, where "rationalized production units" emulate factorylike conditions, most clerical workers in North America do not occupy positions in large information-handling organizations such as banking and insurance firms. (In such settings, in fact, their jobs are likely to be highly rationalized, routinized, and organized by technology.) Instead, large numbers of clerical workers carry out their jobs in small organizations with skeletal front-office staffs. For example, in the sheet metal shop, the repair shop, and other small organizations included in this study, a single female clerical worker at each site handled company correspondence and collateral duties. These included tasks executed frequently by manager-owners, such as scheduling the work carried out by the roadmen, billing customers, and ordering supplies. Lowe (1987) states:

> It is useful to view the small, traditional office and the huge modern bureaucracy as polar ends of a continuum along which various technological, organizational and managerial innovations in the realm of administration can be placed over time. Thus, even though the machine-related jobs that gave rise to the most monotonous, restrictive and unrewarding employment conditions were relatively few in number, a much larger number of clerical jobs were . . . [only] partially affected by the broad thrust of workplace rationalization (198).

Although the small office has been affected by both the new technology and "the rationalizing effects of the administrative revolution," it differs from the large, bureaucratic firm in the way in which clerical work is organized. We should keep this distinction in mind as we turn to a discussion of young clerical workers in banks and insurance firms.

In some but not all cases, as we will see, young workers moving into clerical positions in large insurance and banking corporations face severe restrictions on their autonomy and their opportunities for advancement. Working conditions for clerical employees may or may not be consistent with Braverman's thesis that office work has been "massified" to resemble production line activity in factory settings. As Mortimer and her colleagues (1986), Hall (1986), and others have pointed out, one must look carefully within occupations and firms to examine possibilities for job task diversification and enrichment, as well as differences in the authority and reward structures available to jobholders.

BETTY:
    CUSTOMER INQUIRY REPRESENTATIVE, MIDLAND BANK

Betty began her part-time job at the downtown headquarters of Midland Bank by attending an orientation session for new employees. The session began at 9:00 A.M. after all new workers had been photographed and fingerprinted for the bank's personnel files. The orientation was designed to provide a picture of the bank's employee benefits program, its organizational structure, and its evaluation, promotion, and reward schemes.

During this presentation, new workers learned whom they should regard as their trainers and supervisors and how the bank was organized. The organization's structure was portrayed not as a coordinated work process, with each department making a particular contribution, but rather as Betty Henning, accounting supervisor, Al Mann, security, and other individuals who were in charge of the various bank units. When the trainer flashed a slide picturing the key people who constituted the staff in Betty's unit, the customer inquiry department, she remarked, "Listen to Jeanne . . . [the department supervisor] . . . smart lady, you'll learn a lot from her." In this manner the organization's view of the work process was made explicit to the new recruits. This view, however, was not focused on how an individual's or a unit's activity was related to that of other offices in the bank. Instead it was constructed to show the bank as a hierarchical arrangement of individuals with different titles, responsibilities, and salaries.

At another orientation meeting later in the same day, Betty met with Nancy and Vera, her two immediate supervisors. During this session, which involved only new workers hired in the customer inquiry department, Nancy and Vera reviewed policies covering salaries and procedures. Time sheets, procedures for taking sick leave, the salary schedule, and training procedures were described. Attendance, including policies governing tardiness, absences, and breaks, received most of the attention in the supervisors' remarks. Workers were told that they would be not continued on probation beyond the usual six-month period if they were late or absent more than four times during the initial six-month period.

The rest of the meeting was focused on the training period. Each day over a three-week period, new customer representatives were quizzed on aspects of the bank's policies and procedures, including methods for taking sick days as well as procedures for handling customers' queries. Quizzes were administered after a period designated for study and review of assigned materials, and trainees were expected to achieve scores of 85 percent or better. The first day's quiz, for example, covered knowledge of the organization's key people. Time to study for these quizzes was given on the job, but trainees also were instructed to take about an hour and a half at home to consolidate their understanding of the material. In other words, they were given homework assignments.

Finally, new workers were introduced to the Star System, a computerized monitoring device used by the bank to supervise and regulate the flow of work. This system provided information to assist managers in scheduling Betty and her co-workers to cover periods of greater or lesser work volumes during the day. The major task handled by Betty and her co-workers as customer representatives was to answer incoming calls from customers, who typically wished to find out the balance in a checking or savings account, to determine the reason for an overdraft charge, or to stop payment on a check. The bank's computing system recorded the number of telephone calls handled during the work day by individual employees, the length of each call, the number and length of pauses in individual conversations with customers, and the like. On the basis of previously analyzed similar information, supervisors in Betty's department developed performance standards to cover the pace of work. New workers were told that representatives were expected to handle twenty-six calls per hour.

Betty's initial training sessions left her enthusiastic but understandably apprehensive about her capacity to do well at Midland. At eighteen, she was the youngest customer representative by nearly five years. Yet despite her initial concerns, Betty was viewed by her supervisors as excelling in her position, although neither she nor any of her co-workers regularly achieved the benchmark number of calls per hour or received ratings higher than three out of five. This was one of several inconsistencies that we observed between stated bank policy and actual bank practice.

Job Task Technology and Patterns of Authority

The training sessions on Betty's first day of work at the bank were the most sophisticated and most detailed orientations we observed for the workers who participated in this study. As the following discussion will make clear, job task technology, patterns of authority, and the reward system, although highly bureaucratized, were not as rational as the bank's use of technology in monitoring productivity would suggest. Instead they were tied to the reality that the positions held by Betty and her co-workers were dead-end jobs, cut off from other areas in the bank that would allow mobility in the organization.

In Betty's job as a customer service representative, task technology was governed by the pace of work, particularly the volume of telephone calls handled each hour by Betty and her co-workers. The volume of calls was expected to increase over the first six months of employment. Job task technology in this case was tied intimately to the authority structure—in the case of Midland Bank the two are inseparable—and for that reason both are discussed in this section. Vera, one of Betty's supervisors, put it this way:

> We have a requirement of twenty-two to twenty-six calls an hour. They . . . [the representatives] start at anywhere from fifteen to eighteen . . . [calls] the first month, then they go up to nineteen to twenty. So it's not something we expect immediately. We give them a good six months to really get ahead, because the more confidence they get, naturally, the more times they are plugged in.
> . . . They are going to get these calls promptly. If they know the job, . . . naturally, gradually, once they learn everything, it [i.e., the pace of work] . . . will pick up.

Calls were distributed among the five or six representatives on the floor by an automated distributor. During the first six months on the job, Betty and her new co-workers were monitored regularly by one of three immediate supervisors; through the bank's computerized Star System, the supervisors, undetected by the representatives, could listen in on telephone conversations whenever they wished. According to one of these supervisors, this method of monitoring yielded different kinds of information:

> In monitoring, we pick up different things, such as the type of call, her answer to the call, the content of a call, the timing, her voice, tone, the service she gives. Then we have what we call a "miscellaneous" . . . [category], such as using correct procedures.

In addition to providing accurate accounting information and the like, the customer service employees' adherence to "correct procedures" also involved obtaining proper identification from the customer before providing information and maintaining an "appropriate" number of conversational pauses. Correct procedures were necessary to maintain the bank's security system.

> We, as a bank, naturally are confidential, so we don't give our information . . . [to just anyone]. Customers have to identify their account, and our branches have to give a code that we set

up, or we don't give them any information at all. Also, we monitor out calls—whether they are personal or business. After hang-up time, we also put on . . . [the rating sheet] whether they are filling out forms, if there is unnecessary talk, or if they are just idle.

Although Betty was perceived by all three supervisors as "exceptional" after little more than one month on the job, they only mentioned her skill with irate customers and her ability to handle the technical details of the job as indicators of her "exceptional" skills. Further, and most significant, they were reluctant to give her an overall rating of anything above a 3, which indicated that performance was merely "acceptable." They explained this practice by saying that Betty was still asking questions of her supervisors when certain issues came up. It appeared to us that rating scales in fact were simply a vehicle to provide an outward show of rationality in evaluating new employees. To differentiate among them by providing accurate and just performance reviews would have had the effect of raising expectations for advancement, when in fact no pathway for promotion was open to these women.

At the telephone, where she spent her day, Betty had access to a computerized fund of customer account information. When the computer was "down," however, as it usually was for some part of each work day, Betty was forced to use microfiche cards. Microfiche data typically were incomplete and frequently did not provide the most recent account activity. Thus information regarding overdrawn accounts, stop payments, and the like could not be provided accurately while the computer was not working. Representatives, including Betty, were cautioned not to tell customers that the computer was unavailable, for fear that customers might develop a lack of confidence in the bank. A frequently occurring theme in Betty's occasional asides to her co-workers concerned the difficulties of handling customers' queries and problems with the insufficient information provided by the microfiche. Thus not only did the bank's computer system exert tremendous influence on the manner in which Betty's performance was evaluated; it also was critical in regulating the pace of her work. More calls could be processed when Betty was obliged to respond, "Our activity files are unavailable now. Can you call back in an hour?" This was the request usually made of a customer if the computer was down.

Betty's work was regulated tightly by the technology of her job. Her breaks were taken at four-hour intervals, and she was given a forty-five minute break for lunch. Although their telephone activity was monitored constantly, Betty and her co-workers were allowed some measure of control over the pace of the work. Customer representatives could simply unplug their telephones to avoid incoming queries. They could cover their "unplugged time" by taking more time than might be necessary in filing reports, stuffing envelopes, and handling other paperwork. As might be expected, "unplugged time" was not well received by supervisors.

After two months on the job, Betty was not only bored with her work; she also was extremely unhappy about what she regarded as the bank's rigid enforcement of rules regarding absences and lateness. After ninety days, Betty had called in sick once and had been three minutes late to work on two different occasions; these incidents placed her on a list to be "counseled" by her supervisors. For Betty, being an employee of the bank was like being back in school. Although she expected the bank to be conservative, she did not expect her supervisors to be strict and distrustful. The following statement reflects her observations on the authority structure in the bank:

> Employees are assigned to seats at work, like in school. Employees are not permitted to receive personal telephone calls, ... and [telephone] lines are ... monitored.

Not only were calls regulated; behavior in the office could be scrutinized by supervisors, who had placed specially ordered glass panels on their office doors to allow them a clear view of office floor activity. Although standards were established for the minimum numbers of calls per hour, and although each employee knew how close she was to the standard, only two or three of them (not necessarily the same individuals each hour) achieved their quotas.

After four months, Betty expressed her strong discontent with working conditions at the bank. Although she was able to identify sources of dissatisfaction, she was unable to link these areas of concern either to the working conditions at the bank or to the larger societal issues related to clerical work in large organizations. Her unhappiness centered on three dimensions of the bank's authority structure: the lack of trust between supervisors and employees, the expectation of strict adherence to bank rules, and the excessive number of rules. The interviewer summarized Betty's comments as follows:

> On Not Being Trusted. "I've never had anyone not take my word for things before. No other place of employment treated

me this way." (She had worked at Burger King for three years before taking the job at the bank). . . . "[Here] I get paid $3.75 an hour not to be trusted."

On The Bank's Strict Adherence to Rules. "I was written up as tardy after being only three minutes late for my shift. This was one of two of my tardy citations. The other I got after getting stuck in the snow on the way to work." Bank rules hold throughout the corporation, but some areas enforce rules more strictly than others. Betty claims that the telephone inquiry area is particularly strict, as evidenced by counting three minutes late as being tardy. "They stick to the rules like glue."

On Excessive Rules. Besides performance quotas, promptness and presence at work are critical performance criteria. "That's okay, but only three absences and three tardies are allowed during the first six months of work. The fourth violation in either of these areas means I'm subject to termination. My performance quotas are expected to average 22.7 calls per hour. I've sometimes rushed through a conversation with a customer just to keep under the wire."

Betty was especially disturbed about her treatment during the week she was ill with the flu. She had taken three days off work, Tuesday, Wednesday, and Thursday, which the bank viewed as a single "occurrence." On her first day away from work Betty called the assistant supervisor, who told Betty that although she had experienced similar symptoms, she had come to work anyway. Betty remarked to the observer that this was probably how she had caught the flu.

The bank called Betty at her parents' home on her third day absent from work. Betty, however, had been living with her boyfriend at his mother's house. After her brother answered the telephone at Betty's family home and told her manager that she wasn't home, her mother telephoned Betty's boyfriend's house to let her know. Betty immediately called the bank back and was told that a doctor's note was expected as a verification of her illness. Betty said that she hadn't seen a doctor both because she couldn't afford it and because she believed the illness would simply run its course. She offered to come to work and was told that it wasn't necessary, but that she was required to have a doctor's note. Betty took herself to see a doctor and obtained a note. As a part-time employee, she had no medical insurance coverage or compensation for days absent due to sickness. For the entire period of her employment at the bank, Betty continued working about thirty-five hours each week. Only six of her co-workers were officially working full time, although most, like Betty, worked from thirty-five to thirty-seven hours per week.

Job task technology and the reward system were linked more intimately at Midland than in any other setting observed in the study. In their conversations with us, Betty's supervisors frequently referred to Betty's engaging personality and to her slightly offbeat mode of dressing, but they made no effort to convey that Betty's enthusiasm was cherished or even that her work was a credit to the bank. Rather, virtually every communication from her supervisors carried a punitive message. It is probably true that financial institutions are likely to erect a complex and bureaucratic set of regulations to govern employees' behavior, just as they do to govern the work itself.

The Reward System

Although the bank's policies on salary increases were tied explicitly to performance reviews, which occurred at ninety days, six months, and one year after initial employment at Midland, the reality was that all hourly, part-time employees appeared to receive similar ratings, which hovered at the midpoint on the scale at ninety days and again at six months. Most of these workers were no longer employed at Midland one year after being hired.

Thomas Stanback, in analyzing practices encountered in service organizations such as banks, insurance companies, and other large organizations in this labor market sector, notes that job sheltering through a range of job protection mechanisms (a concept discussed in chapter 2) is absent in most service organizations. Unlike jobs in the fading manufacturing sector, jobs in the service sector are unlikely to be protected by "union membership, licensing or accreditation or by virtue of employment in large organizations operating under conditions of explicit work rules related to seniority and other rights to jobs, promotions, pensions, and the settlement of disputes" (Stanback 1981, 44). Instead these jobs usually are part time; thus earnings are low, and no access is provided to the organization's internal labor market. Of course, firms without real internal promotion opportunities do not describe themselves as such. It is in their best interest to mystify the workings of their internal labor markets.

At Midland, the orientation officer explaining the salary structure for bank employees stated, "In considering your grade level and hourly rate, we compare job responsibilities, not just job titles." She displayed a transparency showing the range of salaries available to hourly personnel and others employed at the bank, and said, "You can't pay the teller as much as you would a manager because he or she has a college education, manages twenty-five to fifty employees, and has more responsibility." Thus the lines between part-time workers such as Betty and managers such as Jeanne, the supervisor, were made explicit both with respect to function (trainer and managers had more responsibility than ordinary workers) and to wages (trainers and managers earned regular salaries, higher than those of part-time and hourly workers). Yet the orientation officer made no effort to explain what kinds of experience, skills, credentials, and cultural capital differentiated hourly personnel from the others or how an employee might move from the status of an hourly employee to that of a regular worker.

The evaluation process was described as "the way you rise up the payroll scale." Categories for evaluation included job knowledge ("how well you know and understand your job"), quality of work, quantity of work, dependability, resourcefulness, attitude and cooperation with co-workers, and customer relations; this last category included not only "how well you get along with customers" but also "how well you dress." New employees were told that they would be given a rating of 1 to 5 on each of the dimensions as well as an overall rating. During their initial thirty to ninety days on the job they would not be eligible for a salary increase, but would be subject to termination if they failed to maintain at least a rating of 2 on all dimensions. Each of the rating categories then was referenced with a statement about the probability of a pay increase. For example, a rating of 3 or above after six months on the job would result in an increase of 5 percent or more. Performance categories or "critical factors" included job knowledge, quality of work, quantity of work, dependability, resourcefulness, attitude and cooperation, and customer relations. New employees were provided with the categories, were given the outline of the rating system, and were told that being "dependable, cooperative, and on top of things" was the key to a high performance rating and salary increase at the end of their first year.

One week after she was hired, we asked Betty about her salary. She was being paid the minimum wage, $3.35 per hour.

> That's what really bothers me. They make you feel so important here at the bank, you know—having this long training session and telling us that managers of the branches will call

us for information and everything, and then they pay us pid-
dlings. . . . But we are learning a lot, and telephone reps get promoted to other parts of the bank.

Thus, initially, Betty was able to rationalize her low salary by
stressing the benefits she derived from her training. This careerist
sentiment ultimately waned, however.

One of the benefits touted to new employees by their trainers
was the bank's system of opportunities for internal promotions.
Jobs were posted, and employees then could place themselves in
position for these jobs after they had been in their current position
for six months or more. Betty's supervisors were the gatekeepers to
these positions.

Although the bank claimed that promotion from one department to another was not uncommon, in fact it occurred only rarely
for the women assigned to Betty's department. Not surprisingly, in
view of the strict adherence to organizational rules and norms and a
climate militating against female clerical workers' access to the
internal labor market, only two employees during their tenure in
Betty's department had actually moved from that department to
other positions in the bank. The supervisors described the process
in a conversation with the interviewer.

NANCY: Most positions they're posting for are busy volume departments like this one is, and they need
the people there and they don't have time to
worry about the tardiness. It's up to the other
area . . . they have the choice of whether they
want to interview them or not. They do not have
to interview them. If they read that . . . [in the
employee's record], they won't interview them, if
they feel that tardiness has been a problem.

INTERVIEWER: Her . . . [Betty's] chances of moving around in
the bank, was she aware that they were not
real good?

GENA: Yes, we keep the department up on policy, so
they know that she had to be out for six months
before she could post.

INTERVIEWER: So she probably wasn't looking internally any
way. But with this posting, if she did get another job, she might have gotten more money as
well, correct?

NANCY: Yeah, usually when somebody posts, they're always posting for a step higher. When you're starting out that low, there's a lateral.

GENA: If someone wants to come to me and wants to job post and they're not eligible, we can write a memo. However . . . I'd explain to my employee also at that time . . . that you've got a problem with absenteeism or whatever, and you would be the last to be interviewed, because the people in the job that are eligible, they are first priority.

Despite the seemingly rational policy at Midland for the promotion and transfer of interested employees, opportunities for mobility were extremely restricted, as implied by Gena's comments to employees whose "absenteeism or whatever," documented in her interdepartmental memos, limited their opportunities.

By the time she had been at the bank for ten months, close to the time she quit, Betty had gained a highly sophisticated view of how the bank's internal labor market *really* worked (Borman 1988). She observed that male messengers such as Reggie in chapter 2, whose job tasks as couriers provided them considerable autonomy, were shown the outlines of a path toward management positions, but that no comparable opportunities were made visible to young women. After nine months of employment, Betty saw clearly that Midland's oppressive authority and reward structures were crushing her spirit, although she did not move to a more political or more structural analysis of her situation. Nonetheless, on a beautiful day in April, Betty went out for lunch and never came back. She then devoted her attention full-time to doing band gigs and arranging light shows for a rock group in which she was lead singer.

MIRIAM: BOOKKEEPING CLERK, RIVER CITY BANK

Miriam would have preferred secretarial work to the part-time position she was given in the bookkeeping department at River City Bank. During the seven months she was employed by the bank, her tasks remained essentially the same: she processed and filed overdraft notices, checks and statements, deposit and withdrawal slips, and statements for personal accounts and occasionally for business accounts. Miriam's department at the River City Bank was responsible not only for processing monthly statements but also for handling customer queries. Miriam worked in the same department as River City Bank's customer service representatives, but she sat on the periphery, at a work table facing away from the computer stations where the representatives worked. Unlike Betty, Miriam received no initial training to acquaint her with the bank's structures and policies. Instead, training for her tasks occurred ad hoc as the nature of the current bookkeeping chore changed. In her case the pace of work depended heavily on the monthly cycle followed by the bank in issuing statements to its customers.

Because she had not received either an orientation to the bank or written materials explaining bank policies, after two full weeks on the job Miriam still did not know such procedures as whom to notify in case of lateness or sickness or even the whereabouts of the employee lavatory. She remained equally mystified about such issues as evaluation and the extent to which employees were permitted to use conversation to regulate the pace of work. She suspected after two weeks of work that conversation was not regarded positively:

> They don't like you to talk here. Whenever Sharon . . . [a co-worker] comes back to work at the files, we talk a little and Margo . . . [the supervisor] comes over and gives us more work.

Although the atmosphere in Miriam's department seemed gradually to lighten, and spontaneous conversations seemed to increase among the workers, these conversations rarely involved Miriam, primarily because of her peripheral location in the work area. In addition, as a part-time worker Miriam was expected to put in five hours of work between 10:30 and 3:30 without a break. Interactions among employees most frequently involved customer representatives; they sat side by side at their respective telephones with the computer screens in front of them, much as at the Midland Bank where Betty worked. Miriam's work, however, confined her to a work station at which she faced not the other employees but an aisle separating her work area from a string of semipartitioned offices.

Job Task Technology

Miriam's isolation was an important aspect of her strategy for regulating the task technology of work in the bookkeeping department. She used mental games such as timing her successive performances of a particular task to regulate the pace of work. Another aspect of her job that contributed to this method was the decreasing amount of time spent in conference with her immediate supervisor. By Miriam's second month on the job, training that had taken up twelve to fifteen hours of her thirty-five hour work week had dropped to five hours per week. By the third month, direct instruction on the job had fallen off completely. Without regular training sessions built into her day and with no official breaks scheduled to punctuate the stream of work, Miriam became increasingly isolated from the flow of activity around her.

During her third month at the bank, a new clerk with similar job responsibilities was hired. Miriam and Donna became friends, riding to work together on the bus and sneaking occasional conversations together over a filing cabinet at the bank. At this time Miriam began seriously to consider another job. When a representative of her employees' group, The American Banking Institute (ABI), discussed the set of course offerings sponsored by the ABI for office workers, Miriam expressed interest and took a brochure. The brochure presented information on two types of courses, all offered as seminars after business hours from 6:30 to 9:30 in the evening. Under the "Functional Courses" category were listed classes in consumer bankruptcy, branch management operations, loan interviewing, selling bank services, and new deposit instruments; other courses grouped as "Banking Support Courses" focused on fund bank data processing, preparing for supervision, and microcomputers in banking. After looking over the materials, Miriam remarked, "I don't see anything here about typing," and put the brochure aside. Of course, she was correct; all the courses assumed an interest in pursuing a managerial position in the banking industry. Because neither co-workers nor supervisors displayed any interest in her development, Miriam remained committed to the notion of a traditional career as a secretary assigned to a "boss" in an organization. Unfortunately, because of her isolation from her co-workers and supervisors, she had no idea of how to move in that direction.

Although she was asked frequently, Miriam typically declined to take extra hours when additional clerical help was needed to generate business statements at the first of the month. The bank's policy regarding overtime annoyed her: "They expect you to stay overtime, don't pay you any extra, and don't even give you a break." Instead Miriam went home every day to practice her typing: "I've got to keep my skills up." After refusing consistently to work after hours, Miriam was no longer asked by her supervisors to put in additional time on the job. Not surprisingly, her supervisors assumed that Miriam was without ambition. They mentioned this point during an interview. Much as at Midland, bank personnel at River City never attempted to provide any social support or to learn about their female workers' ambitions and goals. The prevailing belief held by Miriam's employers is in keeping with traditional labor market economics, which assumes that most people do not have the necessary drive or skills to perform the complex tasks demanded by high-status occupations. Furthermore, when we recall the intimate details that Ellsworth and Lloyd knew about their employees Cal and Andy, it becomes clear that female workers may suffer the effects of strongly negative stereotypes held by their employers.

Patterns of Authority

The poor rapport between Miriam and her supervisor was obvious from the first observation made at the bank. During a fifteen-minute training session, the supervisor did not once establish eye contact and never referred to Miriam by name: Miriam commented on this point during a later observation.

Miriam's relationships with her various supervisors did not improve during the time of her employment. Each side viewed the other with suspicion. Miriam's reluctance to work overtime was taken as evidence of her lack of interest in the job. Because she occasionally gave babysitting responsibilities as an excuse, and possibly because she was African-American, it was even assumed that she had an out-of-wedlock child at home. Miriam had no idea what the bank expected of its employees. "It seems they want you to smile and talk to them a lot. What would I have to talk about with *them?* I come here to do my job." She found it impossible to establish supportive relationships with her supervisors, given her lack of experience and the chilly atmosphere of her department.

Miriam quit her job at the bank to take a job on the assembly line at the major toy manufacturing plant where her mother worked. She reported that she was much happier in this job, primarily because "they let you talk to the person you're working with."

VAL: ADMINISTRATIVE MARKETING SPECIALIST, MIDWEST INSURANCE

There is a prevailing belief that with the advent of high technology in recent years, jobs have become less complex and more routinized. This belief is central to the so-called deskilling hypothesis (Spenner, 1983). Although clerical positions have been viewed by Braverman (1974) and others as among the jobs most vulnerable to deskilling, Val's job, which included composing letters and preparing reports in the agency administration division of Midland Insurance, provided her with a comprehensive overview of her role and responsibilities in the organization. This was the case largely because her immediate superior, Mr. Winn, had defined the training process in advance of her training to include organizational knowledge and related experiences. In addition, among other company benefits, Midland provided compensation for business-related courses offered at a nearby college. During the researcher's interview with Winn, the interviewer noted the following:

> He wants her to understand complete tasks—not just subsections. Along with a co-worker, Val will be responsible for processing... [the files of insurance] agents. Although Val will be able to function autonomously right from the start, it will be about six to eight months before Mr. Winn expects her to grasp the scope of her job. He further hopes Val may develop an interest in moving up in the company. At present, he has an opening available as his assistant, and no one on his current staff shows that they are interested in becoming a manager.

In discussing his plans with the researcher before Val's first day at work, Winn made it clear that he planned to give Val an overview of the scope of work carried out in his entire department. In fact, he met with her immediately after she arrived at the office for this purpose. Winn had been disappointed with a former employee who had occupied Val's position: "After a year on the job, she wasn't able to follow through on projects or initiate work on her own. She needed specific instructions each and every time." In order to avoid this pattern with Val, Winn was determined to see that she worked autonomously from the start.

On Val's first day in the office, the meeting with Winn was the first item on the day's agenda for both the supervisor and the new employee.

> At 8:00 A.M. Val begins the day with a meeting with Mr. Winn, Director of Agency Administration. They meet in his office. He sits behind his large, uncluttered wooden desk. She sits across from him. Mr. Winn wants to explain Midland's distribution system and how they sell insurance. He informs

her that insurance agents are contractual agents—not employees—an important distinction—"Keep that in the back of your
mind." Mr. Winn continues on to explain the licensing process. He is using sophisticated language in this discussion but
occasionally uses analogies such as "the whole nine yards."

"At this point, I don't want to fill your head with a lot of
details that don't mean a whole lot to you . . . I want to give
you work stuff. Hopefully, it will make more sense to you
later." Still he continues to explain. He notes that there are
distinctions between agents, brokers, and part-time agents.
"We handle all administration. We are like the personnel
department, computer department, finance . . . as it relates to
the field. We are here as a service organization to the field. . . .
That's our primary function. You are going to be working hand
in hand with Sally. It's fairly important that you and she have
a good set of cards between you." Mr. Winn then calls Val's co-
worker, Sally, on the phone and asks her to come to the office.

Winn continued this session by explaining to both Val and Sally what
Val's specific assignment was to be. Even though Val would be trained
later by Sally, her co-worker, her training activity was outlined by the
departmental director largely because Winn saw Val as an employee
on a career track in the organization. Contrary to what would be
expected in an organization of this kind and in view of Val's position
as a clerical worker in the firm, Winn provided assurances that he
would use a range of job-sheltering strategies to enhance Val's mobility at Midwest. More important, he made good on his promises.

Task Technology

Despite Winn's careful approach to Val's entry into the organization,
Val's training left her floundering, particularly when her co-worker–trainer was engaged in another, unrelated task and could not rush
to her assistance. Early in her training Val was given an inventory of
sales figures for the previous month. Some of the items were negative numbers, which presented difficulties to Val in carrying out her
calculations. When Val summoned Sally to assist her, she was
unable to gain a comprehensive understanding of the process
because Sally was engaged in covering another set of audits. Sally
assessed the problem, offered a quick piece of advice, and left Val to
carry on. Val's final calculations were off by one hundred dollars.

Frequent interruptions by telephone calls from clients, office chitchat, and traffic around her desk were typical distractions in Val's office, but two factors compensated for these problems. First, Winn's office was next to Val's work area and his office door was always open to her. Thus, during the six-month period in which Val was learning to write and process contracts, Winn suggested that she attempt to gain a comprehensive understanding of the contract format and to consult with him:

> Winn tells Val to take an hour to read the contracts he has given her as models and write out a list of questions, noting, "I don't believe you are going to understand it." He asks Sally to put together a sample set of contracts for general agents, agents, brokers, and an MGI agreement, saying, "Read the contracts. They're extremely boring, but it will become exciting. It's probably where we should have started... [first]. When we get back together, you are going to explain it to me. It's not always this bad. Some days are good. Just ask Sally."
> Val returns to her desk and commences her reading. . . .
> Sally comments to Val, "I never learned about that. All they did was tell me to do it. It wasn't until five years later that I knew what I was doing."

Winn structured Val's training in contracts work much as a teacher would organize a classroom task. Material was assigned, time was given to complete the assignment, and Val was instructed to produce questions about her "lesson."

The second compensating factor was the increasing responsibility that Val assumed in informally training other, newer workers. After Val had worked for several days writing reports to assist agents in their financial arrangements with clients, she was well versed in this set of procedures. When an employee approached Val's desk and handed her a copy of a memo related to these reports, Val spent ten minutes describing the new procedures for filing such documents. Because employees were accessible to one another both by virtue of Winn's open-door policy and by the frequent interaction among employees, an easy exchange of information on company policy and practices was possible. This situation ensured that tasks were carried out relatively smoothly.

Patterns of Authority

The Midwest Insurance corporate offices employed 365 workers in fifteen divisions. Winn, the director of the agency administration division, was in charge of six employees, including Val, who carried out clerical and administrative support activities. In his first conversation with Val, Winn characterized the office's work in this way:

> We handle all administration. We are like the personnel department, computer department, ... finance, as it relates to the field. That's our primary function. As time goes on, you are going to get to know the agents. You may start to feel that someone is a real jerk. But keep in mind, we are here to serve the agents. If they are not there selling insurance, we would not be here either. We will do our best to accommodate the ... [agents in the] field, but we can't violate the rules.

Val's major responsibilities centered on terminating agents, brokers, and part-time agents who had not met their quotas, distributing pension plans, and carrying out the background research activities to support these and related tasks. Because eventually she acquired an intimate knowledge of the agents' activities, she had a real measure of control.

Compared to the jobs of Betty, the customer service representative, and Miriam, the file clerk, both of whom were employed at large banking establishments, Val's position in the office hierarchy afforded her much more control and autonomy. She was expected to take initiative. Winn gave her two pieces of correspondence on her first day, saying, "Val, I am going to give you an opportunity to be creative right off the bat." Although the modifications he suggested to Val were minimal (changing the date and altering a sentence or two), these directions were startling in comparison to the restricted activities and opportunities available to Betty and Miriam. Their work, as we learned in Betty's case, was monitored by a watchdog computer system.

Several factors account for Val's greater autonomy. First, the division in which she worked was smaller than the accounting divisions at Midland and River City; at the latter bank, approximately forty employees worked in a sprawling complex covering most of the bank's fifth floor. Val quickly established working relationships with each of her co-workers, with whom she easily exchanged the usual office banter. Second, it was expected from the start that Val would be given a large measure of autonomy and would be encouraged to understand the connection between her work and that of the agents in the field. Third and most important, her supervisor viewed her as a "management trainee."

The relatively formal, comprehensive, and extended training given to Val reflected the corporation's interest in investing time and money in her training. Winn provided her with an overview of the company, introduced her to co-workers, and subsequently monitored her training activities both to avoid the difficulties he had encountered with poorly trained and uncommitted workers in the past and to groom Val as a future assistant manager. In investing so much time and effort in her training, Winn was responding in large part to Val's educational achievement; her high school average grade was a B in highly academic coursework. Val responded by conforming to organizational goals and procedures; she was still working at the insurance company when the study was completed.

Val attended night school at a local college in Columbus, where she planned to earn an associate's degree in business. Her mother, with whom she was extremely close, had returned to college in her mid-thirties, had completed her B.A., and now was a certified public accountant and president of a family-owned pharmaceutical firm. Val's ambitions also centered on an associate's degree, one that she could complete while working full time. This plan seemed to her to be perfectly congruent with her interests.

Love and romance also occupied Val's time. When the study began, Val had just broken up with her high school boyfriend, who had joined the army and was in boot camp in a distant southern state. A few weeks later she fell in love with Carl, a man five years older who was a foreman in a welding shop. After three months of dating they began to formulate wedding plans; Val began to read *Bride* magazine and to think about the size of her future diamond. When her former boyfriend returned from boot camp for a visit, however, she realized that she had sought the relationship with Carl on the rebound and broke it off. Although her old boyfriend was eventually stationed in Germany, their relationship continued. Many of Val's girlfriends had men in the service and lent each other support.

In addition, Val valued her new independence. She and her co-workers had a particularly close set of relationships that extended beyond the office. Val, Kate, and Jean joined a Swedish Fitness Health Club nearby and went regularly together to aerobics classes after work. On the job, considerable playful banter punctuated the flow of work, as in the following examples:

Sally and Jean talk about upcoming anniversaries for employees in the company and the presents for these people. (Sally serves

on a committee.) Jean looks at the list of employees and says,
"Thirty-five years!" Val says, "Thirty-five. Excuse me, that's
too long! Can you imagine working in a place for that long?"

JEAN: Joe James has been here forty years.

KATE: How many years have you been here, Jean?

JEAN: Eighteen.

KATE: Is that eighteen years too many?

BETH: Kate, be more positive.

VAL: We aren't going to make five years, are we Beth?
How many years have you been here?

BETH: Two and a half.

In addition to easy exchanges such as this about length of service to
the firm, there were also frequent references to family, boyfriends,
shopping trips, and other domestic concerns. These occurred at virtually any juncture in the workday, just as intimate conversation
develops spontaneously around a family dinner table and moves
easily from topic to topic.

Val says, "Are you still waiting for me to do those things or
have you gone on and done it?"

BETH: No, I didn't go on and do it.

VAL: I still have about ten more of these to do. I like this
type (noting the printing on a file). It's really neat.

SALLY: It's called a "display writer."

VAL: How do you know what I am looking at?

SALLY: I can see the Florida emblem. Do you realize that
next month is the time to do my Christmas lay-
away for toys?

VAL: Who thinks about Christmas in September? I don't
think about it until Thanksgiving.

SALLY: I have to buy toys in September to pay them off by
December 15.

VAL: (Using Sally's last name) You must buy a lot of toys,
Samuels.

SALLY: I have to buy for ten kids.

VAL: You should cut down on your list.

SALLY: I did. I cut four of them out.

The women in this department were supported by Winn; his
workplace politics were liberal and perhaps even progressive with
respect to providing opportunities for female employees assigned to

him. As a result, the women felt not only a strong bond among themselves but also an intense loyalty to him. In contrast they enjoyed making fun of the agents who came to their floor for appointments with Winn. The following conversation occurred while Winn was meeting with a general agent in his office:

KATE: If we all got up one day and left, what would they do? I mean all of us—even Winn—what if all of us, even Winn, were asked to work somewhere else for three hundred dollars more a month. Wouldn't that be wonderful? I'm dreaming now.

Winn walks out of his office putting on a coat and saying, "I'll be back."

KATE: Okay, have a nice one. (After he leaves, Kate comments on the agent with Winn when he leaves.) "He looks like a yogurt."

VAL: A lot of GAs look like that.

Playful banter at the expense of other workers is common in the workplace (Roy 1959–60; Borman 1988), but usually joking occurs at the expense of female employees. In a classic example of male workplace humor, Lundberg (1969) describes the construction of a large phallus by workers in a shop. They undertake this project while female employees are at lunch in the hopes that the women will be embarrassed as they walk past the object. The arresting feature of this story (which recalls Giroux's use of the blatantly sexist incident from McLaren's ethnographic description in chapter 1) is that the male researcher, asked by the workers to serve as lookout man to "see the girls didn't get wise," revels in the incident because it illustrates that the men have now taken him into their confidence! Mike Brake (1980) argues that men in Western society cloak their sexual desire for women under the enormous rage they feel toward women. Fearing that their need for women challenges their masculinity, they engage in catcalls and other forms of sexual harassment in the workplace and elsewhere.

Because the major tasks undertaken by Val and her co-workers focused on microscopic details of the agents' lives, it was inevitable that they would joke about a particular employee's age, length of service to the company, or even origins, as in the following conversation:

VAL: Bill Snider was born in... Africa.
JEAN: He's probably the son of a missionary. (They all laugh.)
KATE: You're terrible, Jean.

This incident illustrates that although the women might joke about the agents' appearance, tactics, and other characteristics, they were never observed to make racist or sexist remarks or to carry out elaborate and ugly stunts such as the one described by Lundberg.

Clerical workers remain among the most unenfranchised and marginalized workers in contemporary work settings. The women in Val's insurance department were able to build enough solidarity to recognize and comment about their importance to the company; at the same time they acknowledged the lack of value placed on their efforts, as in the anecdote about the unlikely $300-per-month salary increase. Because it was virtually unique in all the data gathered in this study, workplace solidarity in this insurance office underscores the struggle to build community that clerical workers must wage in most large organizations.

Young female workers in these settings are even less likely than older workers to enjoy the relative autonomy and opportunity for advancement experienced by Val. They are far more likely to encounter the alienation documented in the cases of Betty and Miriam, who were not allowed even to talk on the job without suffering negative repercussions. The major generalization from Kanter's earlier (1977) research in complex and hierarchically organized work settings still holds: Female clerical workers are highly dependent on the structures and careers established by their (usually male) bosses for their well-being and success.

5. THE "NEW" SERVICE JOBS: DEMOCRATIC COMMUNITY OR DENIGRATED EMOTION WORK?

THE CASES OF BETTY, Miriam, and Val presented in chapter 4 illustrated the limits and the possibilities of mobility, the job task technology, and the interrelated patterns of authority and rewards in highly limited clerical occupations. Like most of these young women, many clerical workers in the financial, insurance, and real estate sector of the economy must contend with part-time work, low wages, and limited chances for promotion within their firms.

Nonetheless, the position of workers in this sector is better overall than that of workers in service sector jobs. In fact, as shown in table 5.1, national figures from the Bureau of Labor Statistics illustrate the relative positions of production and nonsupervisory workers across the range of industrial sectors considered in this book. The data in table 5.1 pertain to all such workers in manufacturing, clerical, service, and other sector positions and thus do not necessarily represent the data for young, relatively new employees in these jobs. Obviously, most young workers in manufacturing jobs in 1986 earned less than the average hourly wage of $9.73 paid to all such workers, although Jamie, the materials handler at Selco, earned close to the average hourly wage of $9.19 in 1984. These figures overall show the clear advantage to workers employed in the manufacturing sector; their jobs historically have been protected by unions, federally enforced health and safety legislation, and other

TABLE 5.1

Average Hours and Earnings (in Dollars) of Production or Nonsupervisory Workers in Manufacturing, Retail Trade, Finance, Insurance, Real Estate, and Service Industries

Industry	1980	1981	1982	1983	1984	1985	1986
Manufacturing							
Average weekly hours	30.7	30.8	38.9	40.1	40.7	40.5	40.7
Average hourly earnings	7.27	7.99	8.49	8.83	9.19	9.54	9.73
Average weekly earnings	288.62	318.00	330.26	354.08	374.03	386.37	396.01
Retail trade							
Average weekly hours	30.2	30.1	29.9	29.8	29.8	29.4	29.2
Average hourly earnings	4.88	5.26	5.48	5.74	5.85	5.94	6.03
Average weekly earnings	147.38	158.03	163.85	171.05	174.33	174.64	176.08
Finance, insurance, and real estate							
Average weekly hours	36.2	36.3	36.2	36.2	36.5	36.4	36.4
Average hourly earnings	5.79	6.31	7.78	7.28	7.63	7.94	8.35
Average weekly earnings	209.60	229.05	254.44	263.90	278.50	289.02	303.94
Services							
Average weekly hours	32.6	32.6	32.6	32.7	32.6	32.5	32.5
Average hourly earnings	5.85	6.41	6.92	7.31	7.59	7.90	8.16
Average weekly earnings	90.71	208.97	225.59	230.04	247.43	256.75	265.20

Source: Monthly Labor Review, U.S. Department of Labor, Bureau of Labor Statistics, Table 21 (November 1987):66.

initiatives. Unfortunately, as we have seen, these jobs are on the decline. On the rise are jobs in the service sector, where there is no tradition of worker-organized efforts to assure rights and benefits for employees.

The growth of what economists term "final output" services, such as regular retail sales operations, as opposed to "distributive" (wholesaling) services, is highly contingent on area growth of the runaway producer-services industries (Stanback and Noyelle 1982; Noyette and Stanbeck 1983). Producer services include a widely diverse array of businesses that operate to sustain and support other enterprises. Columbus and Cincinnati have been fairly successful in maintaining diversified economies containing a reasonable share of producer service firms; they have been less dependent on manufacturing operations than Cleveland, Buffalo, or other cities in the northern tier of manufacturing centers. Both Columbus and Cincinnati have succeeded in attracting the development of producer service firms, including administrative support services and research and development organizations such as software firms. These businesses are the key to the related and dependent growth of consumer-directed services, such as those considered in this chapter. In analyses of American metropolitan economies over recent decades, it has become a major proposition that

> the terms of specific metropolitan communities' economic growth and specialization are increasingly defined by different mixes of service (as opposed to nonservice) activities, and that this specialization in export activities influences the occupational characteristics of the . . . [entire] work force and the terms and conditions of employment. (Stanback and Noyelle 1982, 20).

Thus in nodal cities such as Columbus and Cincinnati, which hold regional dominance, "exports are concentrated primarily in distributive and producer services and often, secondarily in other services as well (e.g., nonprofit services, arts, or recreation)" (Stanback and Noyelle 1982, 20). In other words, services often beget other, related services keyed to providing amenities, including good restaurants, art galleries, and major entertainment centers such as King's Island near Cincinnati. In addition, like other nodal places, both cities have relatively large numbers of corporate headquarters. Columbus, as the state capital, also is engaged in the output of public-sector services.

In this chapter I examine work settings in the category of "final output" or personal services sales. This category includes such businesses as specialty retail stores, repair shops, and recreational facilities. Although these services may seem to bear little relationship to one another, they are linked by one common feature: *direct contact with the client or consumer.* Unlike some jobs in the producer services, these jobs demand an orientation to the customer; they require the ability to carry out the "emotion work" necessary to manage complex social interactions as well as task-related technical abilities. This latter group of skills may be routinized and repetitive, as in many fast-food jobs, or quite complex and varied, as in the coin and stamp retailing job to be discussed first in this chapter. Such jobs are burgeoning as the United States passes through what most labor market experts view as a critical juncture in our economic, social, and technological history. In Noyelle and Stanback's terms, "We are witnessing no less than the demise of an earlier economic system, centered on the mass production and mass marketing of industrial goods and the emergence of a new paradigm of economic development emphasizing services, flexible production and customized consumption" (Noyelle 1987, 1). Young workers, along with everyone else in our society, are caught up in this economic change.

ROD: MANAGEMENT TRAINEE, CLIFTON COIN AND STAMP STORE

As many consumers in the United States have attempted to enhance their creative leisure time through "customized consumption," specialty retail stores have mushroomed. In the postwar period from 1948 to 1977, major shifts in the economy, particularly the rise of the dual-earner family, heightened the demand for such consumer outlets as health food stores, spas, and hobby shops. The Clifton Coin and Stamp Store in Columbus benefited so greatly from consumers' interest that Frank, the owner, expanded his operation during our research to include another store. In fact, Rod, his young employee, was made a management trainee and eventually was promoted to assistant manager of the new store.

Rod was being detained in a juvenile corrections institution when he first encountered his future employer. Theirs was the most intense employer–employee relationship observed in the study; it resembled the apprenticeships of colonial times, in which boys and young men worked under the close instruction and tutelage of skilled artisans (Kett 1977). During the study, Rod was confronted frequently by his employer in connection with his use of marijuana and alcohol, was counseled on the weekends, was fired for stealing merchandise from the store, and eventually was rehired and promoted to assistant manager. Through these difficulties both employer and employee struggled with the distinctions between their close friendship and their relationship at work. No doubt the small size of the firm and the specialized nature of the work supported this relationship, but much of the impetus for maintaining it appeared to flow from Rod's desire to please Frank and to succeed at work and from Frank's need in turn to foster the career and influence the life of a young man whose background did not foreshadow success.

Job Task Technology

Greenberger and her colleagues (1981, 1986) argue that service sector jobs provide few opportunities for learning complex social interactional skills or complex skills of any sort. Yet there is little question that Rod's experience as a behind-the-counter salesperson at the coin and stamp store provided a large number of such interactions. Moreover, these encounters with customers were structured carefully by Frank to provide highly interdependent, increasingly complex "lessons" in handling customers, determining the value of merchandise, and observing a code of ethics in connection with purchasing and selling the silver, gold, stamps, and other commodities handled by the store.

The following exchange among Frank, Rod, and a store customer is presented in full to show how Frank routinely structured Rod's on-the-job training during the first three to six months of his employment.

> Customer walks in. Rod gets up to wait on him. The customer is carrying a collection of coins. He wants to get the coins appraised. Rod looks through the coins and sorts them. The customer waits and paces around, looking at the displays. Rod sorts the coins into piles. He looks at each coin. First he opens each envelope and looks at the coin. Then he puts coin back into the envelope. Then Rod begins to take the coins out of the envelopes and leave them in piles on the shelf. Frank walks over to Rod and asks, "Do you know what to do?"
>
> ROD: Look at some of this stuff. I don't know what some of this is.

FRANK: Well, let's look at it.

Frank stacks like coins together and counts them. Rod records the count on an inventory sheet. Both Frank and Rod are looking at and counting the coins.

FRANK TO ROD: Do you want to tell him what happened to that?

ROD: I don't know.

Rod uses the calculator to figure the amount. Counts dimes while Frank explains the worth of one penny . . . [to the customer]. His explanation involves describing differences between steel pennies and copper pennies. The penny in question had been coated but it isn't genuine. Frank proves this with a magnet. Rod posts more figures to the inventory sheet. He uses the calculator to get the total value of the coins.

Frank tells Rod . . . [the results of his calculations]: "Do you want to write this down?" [He dictates a string of figures]: 19 at 35; 4 at (?); (?) at (?); 4.

Frank is interrupted by a customer buying postage stamps; Rod says four at seventy cents. Frank [looks on and says], "Yes, that's OK." Rod continues calculating the value of the collection. What they are doing is counting the number of each type of coin, assessing the coin's value, and recording these data on the inventory sheet.

Frank comes over, points to a pile and says, "That's . . . [worth] $3.50."

Rod records the $3.50 amount on the inventory sheet: $25 minus $4.25. Frank says, "Yeah, write it down." Frank sorts what Rod had finished and what still needs to be valued. He tells Rod to expand the calculation. Rod doesn't know what this means. Frank says to check his work—to check each entry: "For example, . . . this equals that plus the next entry." Rod checks each entry.

FRANK: How did that correspond?

ROD: It's exact: it's right.

Frank, after assessing piles of coins that Rod couldn't figure out, says, "Miscellaneous books and junk—$30.00. Do you want to explain this [points to the inventory sheet] to him?" Rod hands the sheet to Frank. "No, you can." Frank hands the sheets to the customer and says, "You can look at this and if you have questions you can ask." The customer begins to discuss the value of certain coins. Rod helps to look for the coins in question. . . . Frank continues to discuss the value with the customer.

CUSTOMER: What is the value of the total collection?

ROD: "$264.00. Do you want to sell them all?

CUSTOMER: I'm going to see one more dealer. If the price is about the same, I'll come back. Is that price only good today?

ROD: If the silver price is the same, we will buy it at the same price.

FRANK: We buy 98 percent of what we see. You could have saved your time and ours by going some where else first.

CUSTOMER: Well, then, I'll be back. If I knew this I would have gone somewhere else first.

Rod smiles and says, "It happens all the time," and helps the customer package up the coins. (The customer leaves).

Frank hands Rod a sheet of paper. "Gonna skip the good morning stuff. When you get to the customer, you've got to separate the gold and silver, plated and . . . [other] stuff. Separate them into groups. . . . What do you separate gold into?"

ROD: 10, 14 . . . [carat].

FRANK: Others . . . Then [you] test the '10' ones that aren't marked. Don't trust your eyes. It's this level of detail put down in your own words that counts. What would number 3 be?

Rod: Weigh it.

FRANK: Good. Weigh and record on a pay out slip. OK, what's next?

ROD: Convert to pounds.

FRANK: How?

ROD: Multiply by 0.643.

FRANK: Put an example in there. After you convert to pennyweights. Then what?

ROD: Multiply—calculate—prices to be paid to each group.

FRANK: Where do you get the prices?

ROD: Front of [the] sign [on the shop's information sheet].

FRANK: Do you want to put in an example?

Frank calculates an example. "When it comes to taking the customer's money or paying out our money, calculate twice. If payout has more than two items, repeat the calculations. Any time you have a doubt, take the item that is lesser. If you have one answer and then another, do it a third time to get the same answer. If you can't figure it out, holler for help. You don't calculate it at the register. [This is]... how you establish your authority.... When I say it's yours, you... [the customer] can take it.... Make full calculations to your satisfaction the second time. If you pay it straight, I have to trust the customer. If you count it out like I told you, I'll support you.... It has happened before. While they are filling out the payout slip, you take the gold.... They feel much better if it's not in front of them.... If I have a diamond to the scope, the customer is right behind me because they've heard stories about switching. Tell them just what you are going to do.... Are you falling asleep?"

ROD: No, but in about an hour...

FRANK: Repeat groups of silver. Sterling, plated, and foreign coins.

ROD: I don't do those yet. Tell me about it when I do.

FRANK: You want me to tell you about it when you are with a customer?

ROD: No, I'm going to let you do that.

FRANK: You are? Then what do I need you for?

ROD: OK. Give it to me. I'll write it down.

Frank continues the lesson by digressing into how to write an outline. Insists Rod write down information in outline form. Gives rates on foreign coins. Tells Rod to go to sleep earlier. Rod says he did. Frank says 1:00 is not early, it's a wee hour. Frank reviews procedures, asking Rod to provide answers and calculates examples on the calculator.

As is clear from this sales interaction engaging Frank, Rod, and the customer and from the subsequent training session with Rod and his mentor, work at the Clifton Coin and Stamp Store involves what Norwegian work redesigner P. G. Herbst (1974) terms "research-type" learning approaches. The tasks of ascertaining the legitimacy and value of coins, sorting the coins, approaching the customer with conclusions about the merchandise, and closing the sale are what Herbst calls "indeterminate tasks." In this case and in most transactions at the shop, as Arthur Wirth (1983) explains,

there may be a given initial situation and a required outcome and the problem or unknown factor is *the means* to use to get from the initial state to the outcome. For example, when the engine room of a ship... may need to be cleaned... the method

... may be left undetermined... if the crew is permitted to create its own task force which will take initiative in reaching the goal (174–75).

In the coin and stamp store incident, Rod was provided with some strategies for completing the purchase of the customer's merchandise; he was ultimately responsible, however, for devising the specific means to solve the interpersonal and technical problems associated with these transactions. Thus Rod's job tasks, in Herbst's terms, were indeterminate.

Particular democratic principles must be followed in order to structure workplace tasks with indeterminate outcomes: tremendous importance is placed on individual responsibility and autonomy. Indeterminate job tasks contrast with determinate tasks, for which "methods are prescribed in detail and executed under bureaucratic scrutiny" (Wirth 1983, 175). These latter production-type tasks are characteristic of a "Taylorist tradition in industry;" they also parallel the manner in which schools traditionally have organized teaching and learning. Although the considerable variation in school organizational features and in teachers' personalities may modify learning structures, schools assume for the most part that learning will result in what Herbst terms "specified, predictable outcomes." In virtually all school settings, teachers are pressed to "teach to the test"; they often narrow the scope of legitimate school learning to encompass little more than filling in the blanks on worksheets and memorizing "facts." Engagement in the informal learning of the "hidden curriculum" further constrains students' views of the limits and possibilities of relationships between their own interests and what goes on in schools. In the coin shop the informal curriculum in essence was the system of expectations for behavior, such as getting enough sleep before coming to work. In this case it was woven skillfully here into Frank's "lesson" about establishing the value of coins.

Frank consistently but gradually shifted responsibilities such as using the calculator and the shop's information sheet, in a manner that increased the complexity of Rod's job-related skills at a pace the younger worker could handle. As illustrated in the previous incident, Rod felt free to negotiate the amount and types of responsibility he was prepared to take on. Thus, for example, when Frank began to explain differences among sterling, plated, and foreign coins, Rod responded "I don't do those yet" and asked Frank to hold off on the "lesson." Of course the discussion didn't end there;

it was agreed that Rod would learn about foreign currency then and there. In keeping with Herbst's "research-type" learning approaches, for the workplace to keep pace with technological and social innovation, the fundamental qualities of democratic communities must be in place. These qualities are dialogue and respect for individuality. The coin and stamp store was singular as a work setting because respect, as well as the opportunity for dialogue, were highly routine and were taken for granted.

The Authority Structure

Not surprisingly, given his commitment to his young employee's training on the job, Frank was consistently clear about his organization's authority structure. As is true generally, the rules governing Rod's behavior at work were clarified when Rod violated the store's normative practices. This occurred frequently throughout the time of his employment at the store.

At the onset of his employment, Rod upset his supervisor because of his difficulty in maintaining his scheduled hours. For example, Rod was disappointed when his request to come in late to work after the Independence Day holiday was denied. He perceived that this denial would put a damper on his plans for celebrating the holiday into the late hours of the night. Throughout the first three months of his employment, Rod infuriated the assistant manager by showing up when the store opened instead of fifteen to thirty minutes earlier, as agreed. The assistant manager had emphasized earlier to Rod that it was important to come in early. Rod did not adjust his schedule until Frank told him that he *must* arrive earlier. Considerable attention was paid to the young worker's personal well-being as well as to his training in abiding by the rules. Thus it was often difficult to see a prescribed form developing between superordinate and subordinate roles.

In fact, roles and rules in this small retail shop seemed to be arbitrary and flexible at the same time. Frank expected Rod to develop a sense of loyalty to him and to take initiative in learning the business; such an expectation reflected a relationship that was more fitting to a charismatic authority structure than to a rational–legal arrangement. A charismatic authority structure relies on personal qualities and relationships to elicit allegiance, whereas a rational–legal organization is characterized by reliance on a posted set of rules and regulations. In view of the democratic community established by Frank in the coin and stamp shop, Frank's expectations for Rod's behavior do not seem surprising. Although Rod appreciated that his job compared favorably to those held by friends employed in fast-food establishments and other "dead-end" organizations, he was reluctant to take on too much responsibility. Instead he looked for opportunities to lighten the job when they presented themselves—chatting with customers and friends who visited or staring out the window at the pedestrian and automobile traffic. After several months had passed, Frank despairingly reassessed his approach to training Rod. He decided that he would have to become more directive, because Rod had not shown an eagerness to wait on customers; nor had he learned how to stock the store and to develop other skills on his own. Essentially, Frank wished to replace spontaneity with obedience, reducing the opportunity for indeterminate problem-solving tasks and increasing the frequency of Tayorlist-type determinate tasks.

Frank's most articulate and most thorough statement on the moral authority that he wished to see governing relationships at the store was provoked by Rod's enormous breach of his employer's trust—theft of store merchandise. Frank saw himself as a man with serious responsibilities to his family, but also as one whose devotion to Rod was strong enough to challenge his loyalty to his own kin.

FRANK: Now his attitude, it is very difficult for me to differentiate on what I would like to see versus what I am seeing. It's the objective part. I have to rise above the situation and look at it objectively. I feel that I had been used at the time he lost the job. I feel . . . [now] the situation is changing, and I feel he understands that all I want him to do is to learn something and survive as a consequence of that. That's the only reward that I would need from him is success, OK. I believe that he now accepts that is the only thing I want from him and he is willing to work. Because on two separate unrelated, uncoerced occasions he said, "I would not steal from you again."

INTERVIEWER: He has initiated that? Uh huh.

FRANK: Now . . .

INTERVIEWER: And you believe him?

FRANK: I am willing to give him the opportunity to demonstrate such. What I did was I had a very serious conversation with him. Twice I told him what I expected from him, once when he started working permanently and then a second conversation to clarify the drug situation, because once Craig [the assistant manager] decided to accept the offer of starting his own business, that made Rod a candidate for the permanent job [as assistant manager], so I had to explain to him one thing. I said, "Rod, you must not confuse me as your friend and me as your boss." There are two different sets of cir cumstances, and I went into each in detail. I said that there are things that I will forgive you as your friend but I cannot forgive you as a permanent employee. The thing I could not forgive you as a permanent employee is drug- or alcohol-impaired performance, drug- or alcohol-impaired learning ability, drug- or alcohol-impaired dedication in learning. Gee, I am saying a whole lot, ain't I. [I said to him] I cannot have you being late: not only must you be here and learn, but... [you must also] generate revenue. You have to be worth your stay here. If you are just here and just doing a job but not learning to know it completely and thoroughly, you are not performing what I am expecting you to do. If that is related to drugs, I don't want you here. If you steal, then I can't have you as a person who endangers the whole corporation, because now the situation is different. You are not peripheral anymore; you are now in the core of decision making; you can do severe harm; there ain't no games any more. I am never going to allow you to endanger this corporation. This is where the limit is, you cannot be forgiven for that.

INTERVIEWER: By you, his boss?

FRANK: It really rises above me, see, because I have a duty to perform, and the duty is to go and to support my family, and if he endangers that base, I have no choice but to remove the danger, period.

INTERVIEWER: Are there other major shareholders who have decision making in that?

FRANK: It's just me. There is another shareholder, but it is an incidental percent.... [So, I have been clear in saying] "I may forgive you certain things as a friend, but there are certain things I can't forgive you as a boss." ... I want to differentiate how sometimes I would be artificially at work against him because the customer relation demands that and explained that it is not really against him and so forth and so on. I outlined what I would want as a permanent employee, and then it came to the point where he must have that drug habit completely gone because it showed me the difference between when he is on it and when he is not. His inability to verbalize comes from the fact that he smokes (marijuana). There is a certain lethargy; there is a certain inability to verbalize; there is no initiative taking. I said, "You have a very good capacity to learn, and that capacity must exist fresh and clear, because what it is that you are learning must be yours and never distorted, so you know what it really is, so you can count on it." So I said, "You have to choose by March 1, 1984: Do you want your marijuana, your booze, and your freedom? You take it. But if you want to work here, then you must satisfy me in the next three months that you are controlling your drugs ... and this is how I am going to judge: how you talk, how you behave, how you man-age your personal and financial affairs, how you settle debts and all that. I will watch how you are doing. How.. . you solve your problems, how you decide, how you save money, how you think of the future, all this changes as you get off drugs.... You can just tell me that you quit and won't smoke again ... you can do what you want."

Frank's views of Rod's obligations to the firm were influenced profoundly by his determination to see Rod "learn something and survive." Nonetheless, Rod's abuse of alcohol and drugs had endangered "the whole corporation," an entity that included Frank's family as well as the shop's employees and shareholders. Because Frank defined his management of the shop as a sacred "duty to perform for his family," Rod's violation of trust became more than a simple act of insubordination, a major felony, or other kind of bureaucratic or legal offense.

Frank persisted in his devotion to Rod's ultimate salvation from himself despite his family's difficulties with the relationship. Frank's sixteen-year-old son, a member of a Christian youth group, referred to Rod as "the drug addict," Frank's wife requested that Rod be excluded from the firm's corporate dinner party; she was convinced that Rod had hurt her husband mercilessly, an injustice she could not bring herself to overlook. Frank's own persistence in supporting Rod appeared to be linked to what he viewed as the "value of mothering," a role that was tied explicitly to his own early aspirations to "change, teach, and influence people for reasons of pride and immortality." He saw himself treating Rod as his own, a commitment that was "feminine" and which, like much that he valued as "women's simplicity," was in and of itself "very rewarding."

The Reward Structure

Becoming a shareholder in the firm through its profit-sharing plan was one of the immediate benefits in Rod's compensation package. In addition, he was able to purchase resale items in stock in the shop at cost for his own use. Finally, he was at liberty to retrieve any material, such as diamond chips, that came into the store but was not routinely resold. Frank estimated that this last benefit netted Rod an additional $20 per week. When Rod was first hired he worked part time at the minimum wage for about twenty hours per week. After he was rehired in February 1984, he received $4 an hour and was negotiating for a raise when we left the field in June of that year.

When Frank was asked what would determine that Rod was eligible for a raise, he mentioned a willingness to accomplish goals without being told explicitly as evidence of Rod's effort to achieve a "greater goal or purpose." The other quality mentioned by Frank seems to correspond well to his emphasis on a problem-solving orientation to tasks in the shop:

> The other . . . [quality] would be the amount of learning and explanation that he demands . . . [from Frank] in asking ques-

tions ... [such as] "Why are you doing ... [the task] this w⌐
"Why is this that way?" or something like that.

In Frank's mind, Rod's acquisition of strategies for managing th⌐
indeterminate tasks associated with closing a deal was equated
with acquisition of the skills commensurate with a high level of job
performance and with giving evidence of such performance.

DEBBIE: RECEPTIONIST, SWEDISH FITNESS

Debbie worked part time as a receptionist at a large,
constantly busy health spa. Unlike Rod, who was dependably res-
cued, monitored, mothered, and coached by his employer, she
appeared to be always at the mercy of a supervisor who routinely
bullied her and the spa's other female employees. Although
Swedish Fitness salons are linked to a national corporate structure,
management of individual centers appeared to lack uniformity.
This situation may have been a result of the fluctuating fortunes of
the spa business at the time of this research.

Debbie was one of six new employees hired by the manager of
the suburban Swedish Fitness Center in Columbus, where this
research took place. This employment boom was brought on by the
acquisition of another health club chain; traffic doubled as members
of the now-defunct club took up membership in Swedish Fitness.
Along with Debbie, the manager also had hired two salespeople to
promote additional memberships, another receptionist, and two
instructors. Two of these new employees had had previous experience working for other health spa chains. The manager, Cindy, had
initially worked out Debbie's hours at the spa to accommodate her
request for a five-day-a-week schedule that allowed her to work part-
time hours at the spa to approximate a full-time forty-hour-per-
week job. In the organizational flux that characterized employment
at Swedish Fitness, however, Cindy soon was transferred to another
Columbus-area Swedish Fitness location. She was replaced by Ted,
who had rather different ideas about authority relations as they
extended to setting schedules and defining the employee's role.

Job Task Technology

In her face-to-face interactions with more than four hundred
customers a day, Debbie was expected to provide an orientation to

facilities for new or "converting" customers, to dispense work-
t cards and locker keys, and, most important, to maintain an
pbeat, pleasant demeanor. Ted, the new manager, believed that
emotion management was critical for setting the tone throughout
the spa. He described Debbie as follows:

> [Debbie] is a very pleasant individual most of the time. But
> when she's upset, she's either at one end of the scale or the
> other. There is no middle of the road as far as Debbie is con-
> cerned. If Debbie is happy at the desk, then everybody that
> comes in is going to be happy. She has that type of electricity
> in her personality. If she is, excuse the expression, a bitch,
> then she can really pull everything down. But most of the
> time Debbie is a very happy individual.

Being "happy" on the job was reflected in Debbie's interactions with spa members as they signed in at the reception desk
where she worked. The following interaction occurred at 10:15
after Debbie had been at the desk for more than an hour and had
logged in more than seventy members.

> Another customer walks in. Debbie says, "How are you
> today?" The customer, a man in his sixties, says, "Okay, cup-
> cake, how are you?" Looking at the observer, he asks, "Isn't
> she a sweetie?" He turns back to Debbie and says, "I forget my
> age when I see you . . . you're so tall." He tugs on Debbie's arm.
> She punches him in the stomach.

Banter with sexual overtones, such as this, was commonplace at
the reception desk and throughout the spa. A focus on physical
characteristics dominated many conversations between staff and
spa members and among staff members. It even extended to Debbie's dream life. After cutting back on her fitness routine following
an accident, Debbie remarked, "I had a dream last night that I
weighed 204 pounds. I *know* I don't weigh that much. I don't look
that heavy."

The Authority Structure

Jokes about one's appearance and about flaws or anomalies in
others' physical characteristics predominated in this setting. Management attempted to enforce a number of rules to minimize this

emphasis. Employees were not supposed to date each other; T-shirts or sweats were to be worn by trainers and aerobics instructors; hair was expected to be neat and conservatively styled. All these rules were violated by the employees, however. One man kept his long lock of black hair tucked into the neck of his shirt at the nape; dating couples attempted to be secretive in arranging their dates; instructors were lax in enforcing the T-shirt rule. Although the normative order that management attempted to establish emphasized the importance of managing employees' sexuality, the nature of the work carried out in the spa ran in direct opposition to management's rules. As a result, violations of the normative order by young employees at the spa recurred frequently.

In *The Managed Heart*, her analysis of the commercialization of human feeling, Arlie Hochschild (1983) examines the jobs performed by flight attendants. They, like employees in the spa, carry out "emotion work." In service industry jobs, "feeling rules and social exchange have been removed from the private domain and placed in a public one, where they are processed, standardized, and subjected to hierarchical control" (Hochschild 1983, 153). Workers who hold jobs that provide service to the public constitute fully one-third of the current U.S. labor force, as we have seen. Characteristically, these jobs are held by women, who, in Hochschild's words, suffer the "hidden injuries of gender." These injuries are attached to those of social class, because service jobs are ranked at the low end of the job prestige continuum. According to Richard Sennett and Jonathan Cobb (1973),

> at the bottom end of the scale are found not factory jobs but service jobs where the individual has to perform personally for someone else. A bartender is listed below a coal miner, a taxi driver below a truck driver. We believe this occurs because their functions are more dependent on and more at the mercy of others (236).

Like an airline hostess, Debbie was expected to be "up," to handle sexual innuendoes with equanimity, and to do so for twelve hours at a stretch. Unlike airline personnel, however, Debbie was expected to provide these services while being paid only $3.35 per hour. Debbie's one small advantage, her flextime schedule, was the only "privilege" she had been able to secure. When Ted became her boss, he was appalled by the "casual" scheduling arrangements that his predecessor had tolerated. Ultimately he arranged for Debbie's transfer to another spa to get her out of his hair and to tighten things up. Although Debbie was never evaluated formally, Ted was quite clear in his assessment of her ability to manage emotion work well:

> One time I yanked her into an office when she was having one of her monthly visits from . . . you know, that period of the month when they don't feel real well . . . they don't handle criticism real well. This is when I first came . . . [to the spa], and Debbie and Cindy worked when they wanted to for however long they wanted to. That was their schedule. There was no rhyme or reason to when they worked. . . . So when I came in and tightened up the reins a little bit, tried to make it a little more organized . . . maybe they didn't feel they were appreciated as much as before. That's when I had to put Debbie in her place and let her know this is what we have to do and when we have to do it, and that I do not always say "please" and "thank you" when I want things done. That's because I have a hundred things going at that particular time. It doesn't mean that I don't appreciate it as much as maybe someone else does.

Ted knew clearly that *his* job as manager did not require him to engage in emotion management with his employees. His job was tightening the reins and showing people who was in charge. It was certainly not Debbie's job to set her own schedule. Being happy, attractive, and friendly was labor's job, even during "that period of the month when they don't feel real well." Little regard was accorded to Debbie's emotions; in addition, her authority and even her humanity in these circumstances were denigrated. Because employment opportunities for female workers in recent years have centered overwhelmingly on the development of jobs in the service sector, the obvious concern must be with the quality of female service workers' work lives. As has been shown both in clerical work and in the more "glamorous" health spa setting, females in these jobs receive few material rewards, have highly marginalized status, and enjoy little basic deference from their co-workers for their efforts.

In explaining the lack of what she calls "basic deference" in service jobs, Hochschild (1983) concludes the following:

> Once women are in public centered jobs, a new pattern unfolds: they receive less basic deference. That is, although some women are still elbow-guided through doors, chauffeured in cars and protected from rain puddles, they are not

shielded from one fundamental consequence of their lower status: their feelings are accorded less weight than the feelings of men (171).

During the course of an hour, as described in field notes below, Debbie handled at least ten phone calls, signed thirty customers in or out of the spa, and made five announcements over the public address system, while occasionally interacting with Bill, the assistant manager.

A guy entering the spa asks Debbie, "How are you doing today?" [Another customer] says "Fine" and Debbie gives her a key. The guy asks Debbie "How are you doing today?" Debbie says "Fine." An older woman who has already checked in comes toward the desk. Debbie asks, "May I help you?" The woman says no and points to an older man, who gives her a hug and a kiss.

Debbie gets on the phone and makes a call, and carries on an extended conversation with the person. She laughs as she processes people out two times, then processes two persons in. She processes one guy in and two guys out. Gary walks through receptionist area; Debbie doesn't change her stance or stop laughing. Bill, the assistant manager, comes over and looks at the appointment book. Debbie stops giggling and jots down a few notes. Then Bill walks away.

Debbie gets a card for a woman who is leaving. Debbie gets another call. She answers it and then pages Jennifer to line 1. She returns to her call. A woman comes down and signs in; Debbie takes her card and gets her a key. Debbie says, "I just wanted to tell you. . . . "Then she gets another call. She answers the call and conveys a message to an employee who is four feet away. Then Debbie ends the call.

Two [black] guys sign in and Debbie pages Robbie. Debbie then starts to question how often a black guest comes in. As soon as Robbie comes down, Debbie backs away, and Robbie explains the guest policy. She says to one guy, "You pay to come here, why should he come here for free?" The guys agree, and Robbie lets them through, but says no more after this.

Debbie asks another customer to sign in. She says, "That was Theo, you reminded me of him so I called him." Then Debbie processes two people out. Then she makes the "Buddy Bonus" announcement, the first of the day.

Two program directors stop by to see if they have any appointments. It looks like they had a long meeting with Cindy and Steve. They check the book and Debbie discusses appointments with Glen.

Debbie says, "Hi, Gary [another employee], you going to work out?" Gary says, "Yeah". Debbie says, "You should wait until tonight and work out with me." Gary asks, "Why? Do you need someone to push you through?" Debbie says, "Yeah, I need some motivation."

Steve walks by. He glances over. An older gentleman walks up to the desk. He asks for a tall locker. Debbie says, "That can be arranged." Debbie processes two people out. Debbie walks over to Bill, who is still looking over the appointment book. Debbie laughs with Bill. Then Debbie returns to filing the workout cards.

A woman comes up and spells her name. Debbie comes over to hear, then goes over to the files to get the card. She can't find it, so she asks the woman again. The woman says, "I didn't think you heard me." She spells her name again and Debbie finds the card. Two people that Debbie knows stop by and chat for several minutes. Two people come up to check in. Gary, now off duty, comes up and talks with them. Then another man comes up and Cindy comes through . . . [the group] and looks at his card. Cindy tells Debbie to order . . . another card because the expiration date can't be read. Two other members come up to the desk for a card. Debbie processes them in. One woman has a problem about something.

Gary comes up and gets involved with the woman and brings her up to the main area. Gary tells Debbie to make another "Buddy Bonus" announcement. Debbie says "I will at 3:00." Then she comes over and asks me [the observer] what time it is. I tell her.

Debbie returns to filing the workout cards. A lady comes up and puts her key on the counter. Debbie takes the key and then returns the lady's card. Another woman comes up and has a problem. Debbie pages a program director. A program director arrives and describes some specific exercises to the woman. Debbie files three people out and then continues filing the workout cards. She takes a phone call and then announces, "Will a program director please pick up on line 1?"

Cindy comes over and introduces herself as division manager and asks about the study. I explain, and then I ask how long she has been with Swedish Fitness. She tells me that she has worked herself up from an instructor, so she knows what it is like to be in every position. She has worked for Swedish Fitness for two and one-half years.

Debbie notices a program director lying down in the corner. She announces his name over the PA and then walks over to him. He is lying in the far corner of the spa. While she's over there, three people walk up to the desk, and she gets a phone call. Debbie answers the phone on the far side of the spa, then puts the person on hold and runs back to the reception area. She processes two people out and two people in.

A man comes in and says that he needs a new temporary membership card. . . . She says that she needs to look this up on microfiche. She asks for his name. Then she gets out the fiche and starts to look up his name. Next she gets interrupted by people coming in and calling on the phone. She returns to the fiche each time she completes a transaction. She finds the name and runs up to the manager's area to get the temporary card. She gives the card to the customer, apologizing for the delay. Client stops to tell Debbie that the mike is too loud and she can't understand it when Debbie makes an announcement.

This passage illustrates the constant demand on Debbie to engage in brief but frequently intense interactions with customers and co-workers. It also reveals that the conversations in the spa were truncated and staccato in comparison with the sustained interactions between Rod and Frank in the coin shop. Rather than being sustained, these conversations had an incomplete and disjointed quality. Further, they did not result in the acquisition of increasingly complex job-related skills, as was the case in the coin shop.

Debbie never received the opportunity to view her encounters with customers as an avenue to developing a problem-solving approach to tasks with indeterminate outcomes. Indeed, her customers and co-workers would have been disconcerted if (for example) she had questioned seriously the timing of the "Buddy Bonus" announcements over the loudspeaker system or had challenged the rationale of the sales strategy inherent in the "Buddy Bonus" plan. Likewise, the tendency to question African-American customers but not whites about the potential abuse of the spa's guest policy was never viewed as problematic. Instead, social currency in this setting was cheap and taken for granted. A substantive conversation focusing on social values would have been inappropriate in this setting.

The comparative case studies we have examined in chapters 3–5 demonstrate that manual labor is degraded in the youth workplace less than female labor in particular work settings. In places where young women are employed as clerical workers or emotion management workers, the job task technology, the authority structure, and the reward systems seem to be meshed; accordingly, all of these structures are mystified. This conclusion was revealed most dramatically in the spa setting. The arrival of a new manager deprived Debbie of the one element she had been able to construct for herself in the work setting, namely, the management of her time at work to correspond with regular full-time work hours. Debbie stayed at the spa two months longer before quitting; she remained unemployed for the duration of the study. At that juncture her dreams centered on acquiring a husband and shunning work altogether.

6. CONCLUSIONS

THIS BOOK HAS EXAMINED the work settings and work experiences of young men and women following their graduation from high school or their departure without a diploma. These young workers were participants in a project designed to illuminate the connections between the economy and how individual work lives are constructed in youths' first "real" job. This study explored the day-to-day structure of work for young people whose jobs were located in factories, sheet metal shops, major financial centers, and other businesses. These workers were followed into forty-six work sites over the course of the twelve months the researchers spent in the field. In addition to making observations at work sites during young workers' regular shifts, the researchers also interviewed them and their employers, parents, co-workers, and friends.

Issues surrounding young workers' entry into the labor market are rooted largely in the changing American workplace. Our society has moved from a goods-producing economy to a service-producing economy; this change has altered the fundamental rhythm and character of daily work life for all workers and has placed young workers in unusually disadvantageous positions. Work for the typical eighteen- to twenty-two-year-old service employee in this study required middle-class deportment on the job but paid less than blue-collar work. Even workers whose jobs required more typical blue-collar manual skills were plagued by uncertainties. These young workers feared that production would be cut back or that automation would be introduced to the assembly line, and that consequently they would lose their jobs.

This chapter attempts to derive important themes from the studies of the first "real" jobs held by the young workers whose cases have been discussed in this book. The youths whose jobs and lives were documented during the period of observations and interviews present a wide variety of experiences. It is important to emphasize that in contrast to previous studies of youth jobs (Greenberger et al. 1986), our research demonstrates, for example, that close mentoring and support are not entirely absent from the experiences of young workers. Although workplace experiences vary on this dimension and others, these experiences contain common elements. For example, each workplace is a habitus and a labor market niche with opportunities and constraints for young worker's individual development.

This chapter considers two major themes. The first is related to the social reproduction of labor. According to social reproduction theory, discussed in chapter 1, the habitus of the workplace is the locus for the reproduction of values, beliefs, and behaviors that perpetuate class distinctions from one generation to the next. This habitus includes the workplace subculture, its linguistic code, and the emphasis on critical awareness of workplace and job constraints, on literacy, on other higher order skills, and on exposure to new ideas. The first theme to be considered, then, is how the habitus of the workplace varies across settings. In addition, it is crucial to consider the impact of the workplace habitus on young workers.

The second major theme relates to the youths' personal and social characteristics, such as social class, gender, race, and ethnicity, as well as characteristics inherent in the widespread, negative social construction of youth in our society, which emphasizes youths' naivete and lack of experience. Most of the young people in this study were working-class children of working-class parents. How does social class interact with youths' other traits, such as their inexperience in the workplace? How are gender and school experience—particularly enrollment in the general curriculum as opposed to the academic or the vocational track—related to the amount of autonomy, and opportunities for promotion in the firm? How are these characteristics related to knowledge of rules and to youths' awareness of opportunities or constraints in their particular workplaces? In order to examine these themes I make comparisons across the cases considered in the earlier chapters of the book. These comparisons will allow us to understand how, in the language of labor economics, employees' characteristics mesh with labor market niches, the actual workplaces in which youths' jobs are located.

HOW DOES WORK EXPERIENCE VARY ACCORDING TO THE WORKPLACE HABITUS OR JOB SETTING IN WHICH THE YOUNG EMPLOYEE WORKS?

The workplace habitus includes the social system of values, beliefs, and behaviors that generally characterizes experience for a particular social class (Bourdieu and Passeron 1977). This concept is important in explaining the social reproduction of privileged groups in any society. From a labor market perspective it underscores the fact that certain characteristics, attitudes, and skills are valued more highly than others and that society is willing to pay a premium for those properties in the form of higher salaries and other rewards. This concept, when applied to job settings where young workers are employed, illustrates that some work experiences in particular work settings are more instrumental in providing access to higher-order skills, such as literacy, as well as to the intellectual challenge of new ideas.

In this section of the chapter our discussion of how work experience varies across work settings reviews the major work sites examined during the course of the study. The work sites were located in the labor market sectors currently employing young workers. In the changing economic order, factories and job shops such as the sheet metal shop in Columbus where Cal and Andy worked are on the decline. By contrast, jobs in old-line, traditional service businesses such as banks and insurance firms are on the rise. Other important markets for young workers are those in the new service industry sector, particularly in the so-called burger economy, in health spas, and in specialized retail establishments such as the coin and stamp store. As has been mentioned, fewer young workers will be able to find work in factories and shops, and in the future young workers probably will turn to service enterprises for employment. Among such firms, perhaps the most attractive are those considered in this book. Financial institutions and personal service sales operations are much more appealing to workers than gas stations and fast-food restaurants.

Although Jamie's job as a materials handler at Selco was "boring," as he put it, he was able to vary both the pace and the method of his work. Skill development and exposure to new knowledge, however, seemed limited in this setting. The young employees in Jamie's work crew, nonetheless, built a community and a camaraderie that extended across the factory itself. Jamie participated in a car pool that included workers from other departments; he derived considerable satisfaction and a measure of status from his participation on the company's baseball team; and he made more money than anyone he knew from his high school class (or anyone *we* knew in the study). It is likely that Jamie will remain at Selco, as have his mother and many others from his semirural town for most of their careers.

The sheet metal shop was very similar to the factory in some ways. Rather than being drawn from a particular geographical locale, however, young workers at the sheet metal shop were recruited from a particular vocational school. As a result, at least among the young sheet metal cutters, a community of shared interests, mostly antithetical to the values of the workplace, was created. For example, "long lunches" and late arrivals to work in the mornings eventually cost Cal his job. Although Andy gained considerable experience at the shop, he was not satisfied with the work, primarily because wages were low and there was no opportunity for advancement in the firm. Andy will in all likelihood move on to another shop once he is able to convince a new employer that he has acquired the skills and maturity demanded by the work in that setting. Although Andy desired to change jobs, he does not wish to abandon sheet metal work.

Like Andy, Peter, the appliance-repair worker whose interview we discussed in chapter 2, held little regard for work that entailed sitting behind a desk. Manual labor, or not being in the "brain part" of things, as Jamie might put it, is valued by Jamie, Andy, and Peter. Paul Willis, Peter McLaren, and others would argue that valuing manual labor is a manifestation of their working-class origins. However, it is also true that these workers have greater job security, arguably better working conditions overall, and much higher wages than young workers in the study holding jobs in the service economy. Still, as Andy's supervisor freely acknowledged, the skills and training that young workers had received in high school vocational courses were rarely demanded by the tasks assigned them in the workplace.

In sum, the workplace habitus of factories and shops examined in this study present a mixed picture. In general, linguistic codes are not elaborated or focused on new knowledge. While skill development occurred in the appliance-repair shop and to some extent in the sheet metal shop, skills demanded day-to-day in these settings usually lagged behind those acquired by the young workers in high school.

Young workers in these settings were well aware of internal labor market conditions in their firms. Andy knew that Floyd, the foreman, could not quit his job soon. Jamie knew that Selco's automated production lines would replace employees and threatened his chances for promotion. The habitus of these settings promoted a reasonable amount of valid information about job opportunities and constraints. However, higher order skill development and intellectual challenge were notably absent.

Among all the settings considered in this volume, the coin and stamp store where Rod was employed provided the most supportive ethos and the greatest access to complex knowledge. In this workplace his employer structured Rod's work in a manner that developed an increasingly elaborated set of responses to job tasks. The indeterminate nature of the coin and stamp store's daily transactions encouraged Rod's acquisition of sophisticated knowledge about the value of the store's stock, methods for estimating the value of the customer's goods, and strategies for negotiating a favorable price. In addition to his exposure to cognitively challenging tasks, Rod was supported by a mentor deeply committed to the welfare of his employee, an advantage that assured Rod's sustained development.

Dramatically contrasting demands and constraints characterized the job task technologies, material (and nonmaterial) rewards, and authority structures in workplaces employing young women. The clerical positions held by Betty and Miriam in the two bank settings were especially ill-suited to the development of their technical skills and autonomy. Working part time at the minimum wage further reduced advantages these jobs might offer. Job knowledge was limited and constrained. Recall the limited view of the organizational structure of the bank presented to Betty during her training. Keep in mind the fact that Miriam did not know the location of the ladies' restroom, much less the bank's policies on employee absence, promotion, or transfer. Unlike the young men whose job experiences we have considered, neither Betty nor Miriam remained in her job for the duration of the study. As we have seen, Betty was beleaguered by a highly intrusive surveillance system, while Miriam was likely to receive additional tasks as a "punishment" if she engaged in even limited conversation with a co-worker. These cases illustrate the manner in which employers are likely to utilize highly authoritarian disciplinary strategies with their young women workers. Workers have few choices in such situations; they may rebel, conform, or retreat. None of these strategies offers a particularly advantageous position, however, since young female workers in particular have very little social power. Both young women chose to retreat by quitting their jobs to seek employment in situations that were radically different from the bank.

Social reproduction theories applied to the labor market make assumptions about workplace technology, material rewards, and social relations that do not appear to be valid in the current youth labor market. The assumption that manual labor skills are socially denigrated and rewarded less well than verbal skills is patently false when applied to jobs in the youth labor-market economy. Further, although opportunities to acquire more sophisticated job knowledge may be apparent in traditional service sector jobs, generalizations about the quality of such job-site knowledge acquisition must be qualified. Miriam in her job at River City Bank observed that her supervisors did not like her and her co-workers to talk at all. It is difficult, if not impossible, to acquire higher order skills such as those involved in negotiating or carrying out indeterminate tasks in these circumstances. Clearly, it is not sufficient to consider the workplace habitus alone. In order to understand how the full range of job-related characteristics—the amount of autonomy, opportunities for promotion, knowledge of rules, and so forth—are related to youths' experiences, we must also consider their own individual characteristics as well as those stereotypically assigned to youths in this society.

HOW ARE YOUNG PEOPLE'S WORK EXPERIENCES INFLUENCED BY THEIR PERSONAL CHARACTERISTICS AND BY THE CHARACTERISTICS INHERENT IN YOUTH?

Among the personal characteristics of youths most salient to their work experiences, gender, race, and social class seem most important. Other characteristics, such as exposure to an academic, general, or vocational curriculum while in high school, are dependent on these three traits. Further, young workers are all restricted by our society's negative appraisal of their abilities. Youth as a phase in the life course is widely regarded as a period of floundering. Youths' inexperience and lack of maturity are emphasized by some analysts, while others place extraordinary and, in my view, inappropriate emphasis on white male working-class youths' political prowess (Willis 1977).

Youth as a phase in the life course emphasizes youths' struggle to develop a coherent identity. A clearly important aspect of this development is the construction of an occupational identity. It is important to emphasize that adolescents value work. In fact, success in work is prized more highly than relationships with family or friends, as is clear in empirical studies of contemporary high school seniors documented in the work of Eckstrom and her colleagues (1989). Indeed, if work were not central to the self-esteem and identity formation of young people, it is likely that we might not have observed the exodus from particularly oppressive work settings documented in this study.

As we have seen, young women workers in both traditional and new service jobs experienced the most negative working conditions. We have already referred to the cases of Betty and Miriam, the bank employees who eventually left their positions as clerical workers. The most graphic example of the negative impact of the work environment upon an individual worker in this study was Debbie, the health spa receptionist. Her supervisor, Ted, not only imposed a harsh set of scheduling rules but also openly denigrated his employee in gender-specific terms. Debbie was seen, in Ted's words, as particularly difficult during "those times of the month when [women] don't feel real well." Debbie's ultimate strategy was to retreat completely from employment and, presumably, from the active construction of her occupational identity. After leaving the spa and remaining unemployed for a period of several weeks, Debbie told the interviewer that her current ambitions centered on marriage. She had no plans or desires to gain employment.It is difficult to understand how the moratorium Debbie placed on the development of her occupational identity stemmed from a personal flaw or a more general "floundering" characteristic of all youths. Rather, it seemed an appropriate reaction to the consistently sexist behavior of her supervisor, Ted. Ted's behavior contrasts with the response of Reggie's supervisor at the bank. Recall that Reggie, who often received citations for traffic violations on the job, was accommodated by his supervisor, who desired that Reggie, one of the bank's star football players, stay with the firm. Women, as Hochschild and others have illustrated, routinely experience denigration, especially in the context of new service sector jobs.

While gender stands as the most critical individual factor in determining the locus and nature of workplace experience for young workers, race and social class also have a powerful impact. African-American males who have less than a high school education and who live in inner-city neighborhoods have a severely limited range of employment opportunities, for example. In discussing the impact of gender, race, and social class on young people's work experience here, it is important to keep in mind that we are making generalizations based on a limited number of cases in this study. This book has examined the experiences of eleven young workers who participated in the research I have reported here. Like most of their counterparts among the fourteen additional participants in the study, these young workers came from working-class backgrounds. Among the eleven cases examined closely in this book only two, Debbie, the health spa receptionist, and Val, the assistant manager at the insurance firm, had middle-class origins. A review of figure 2.1 in chapter 2 shows that Debbie's father is an accountant, while both of Val's parents held relatively prestigious jobs. Among the remaining fourteen young workers, only one, an African-American, Lisa, had parents employed in jobs that could be regarded as middle-class. Lisa's father is a manager, and her mother is employed as an elementary school teacher. During the first three months of the study Lisa worked as a dancer at King's Island, a major entertainment complex near Cincinnati. Lisa at the time of the study was nineteen years old and had left Indiana University's program in ballet to gain more intensive experience as a dancer. After the park's regular season ended in October, Lisa found work as an aerobics instructor in a Cincinnati health spa. She quit after six weeks and returned home to Indianapolis. Her plans were to return to Indiana University, although she was not sure about her desire to pursue a career in dance.

Given the rather anomalous cases of both Lisa and Reggie, the African-American employee at Midland Bank, it is difficult to generalize about the effects of race and social class as they interact with gender to determine the nature of work experience for young employees. Both Lisa and Reggie were extremely talented, Lisa as a dancer and Reggie as an athlete. Lisa was one of only three participants in the study whose parents were not unemployed, employed either as manual workers or in low-level sales jobs. However, Lisa's and Reggie's cases both demonstrate that African-American youths' access to employment is frequently channeled through athletics and the performing arts and that these avenues are highly restricted. An extremely small percentage of all youth jobs are in this category. Further, the fact that we were able to recruit only four participants overall (Cindy, Reggie, Lisa, and Miriam) who were African-American underscores the dilemma faced by young workers of color in the United States. Simply put, they have highly limited opportunities to find *any* kind of employment at all in our current labor market economy. Few positions are reserved for them in any but the least advantageous labor market sector.

Overall, social class appeared to have the greatest impact on the aspirations, desires, and plans of the white males in the study. Most of them desired to remain employed indefinitely at the jobs they held during the study. White females, in contrast, held ambitions that were incongruent with their current circumstances. In some cases, such as Betty, the impact was liberating; Betty left her job at the bank to work with a New Wave band. In other cases, such as Miriam, social class interacting with race and gender appeared to foster both rather unrealistic career goals—Miriam desired to be an executive secretary—and an outcome that seemed to foreshadow the intergenerational reproduction of social class—Miriam left the bank to work on the toy factory assembly line where her mother had been employed for many years.

In summary, two sets of findings emerged during the research and the subsequent data analysis. First, as we have seen, the location of the job in a particular sector of the labor market fundamentally shapes the organization of work, including job technology, job requirements, the demand for labor, job values, the reward system, and conflict-resolving mechanisms. For example, clerical work is very different from factory work on a wide range of dimensions.

Second, we have observed that gender has an enormous impact on the kinds of employment opportunities available to young men and to young women. Gender differences in job task technology, rewards, and workplace authority structures are readily observable. We have seen how young men hold jobs with relatively more sophisticated and transferrable technologies, financial rewards, and flexible authority structures. Young women, with the exception of Val, whose training in the insurance firm was geared to managerial responsibilities, were given highly routinized, unskilled, and marginalized or closely monitored roles and responsibilities. Perhaps the most dramatic aspect of how work has been transformed for young women (while remaining unskilled) is in the transfer of traditional female work roles to emotion work. Although their traditional roles as domestic workers placed somewhat similar demands on the women who held these jobs, the relentless and staccato pace of social interaction in a health spa or fast-food restaurant cannot be compared to the rhythm of work in a household setting. Moreover, as we have seen, because of competing and constant demands on workers' attention, interaction in most service-industry workplaces is not conducive to open-ended, indeterminate problem-solving tasks of the kind Rod experienced in the coin and stamp store.

In view of the poor support from most employers, and particularly from schools for young people seeking work, it is important that school policies and practices be formulated to assist youths in making the transition from school to work. We are beginning to see possibilities for what Arthur Wirth has called the effort to "introduce into schools the philosophy and techniques of democratic sociotechnical work theory" (Wirth 1989, 547). Wirth claims that we are at a crossroads in American education. We can either continue to maintain school systems, buildings, and classrooms that perpetuate a "lifeless bureaucratic perfect gaze" or we can turn to a fusion of technology and principles that support school-based initiative, inquiry, and decision-making (Wirth 1989, 547). Wirth argues that schools and classrooms must become learning communities in which teachers are free to work collaboratively, take initiative, and actively utilize computer technologies and methods of cooperative problem solving to construct learning programs. This argument is especially compelling in view of the cases we have considered here. For example, Betty's experience at Midland Bank, where she was subjected to relentless surveillance by the computerized Star System, demonstrates how technology is currently used by some businesses to monitor workers. Betty's observation that the authority structure at work was "like being in school" illustrates how unfortunately clear the connection is between these institutions.

Changes in schools and workplaces are becoming increasingly widespread. This book has documented the price many young workers pay when change does not occur swiftly enough to benefit them. As I bring this volume to a close I can only express my hope that these particular young workers are able to encounter a liberating work curriculum in their lives before too many years have passed.

REFERENCES

Baron, J. and Bielby, W., 1985. "Organizational Barriers to Gender Equality: Sex Segregation of Jobs and Opportunities" in *Gender and the Life Course* edited by A. Rossi. New York: Aldine.

Bernstein, B., 1975. *Class, Codes, and Control: Volume 3: Towards a Theory of Educational Transmission.* 2nd ed. London: Routledge and Kegan Paul.

Bernstein, B., 1977. "Social Class, Language and Socialization" in *Power and Ideology in Education* edited by J. Karabel and A. H. Halsey. New York, NY: Oxford University Press.

Bishop, J., 1986. *Preparing Youth for Employment.* Columbus, OH: National Center for Research in Vocational Education.

Blau, P. and Duncan, O., 1967. *The American Occupational Structure.* New York, NY: Wiley.

Borman, K. M., 1988a. "Playing on the Job in Adolescent Work Settings." *Anthropology and Education Quarterly 19,* 163–81.

Borman, K. M., 1988b. "The Process of Becoming a Worker" in *Work Experience and Psychological Development Through the Life Span* edited by J. T. Mortimer and K. M. Borman. Boulder, CO: Westview, 51–75.

Borman, K. and Hopkins, M., 1987. "Leaving School for Work" in *Review of Research in the Sociology of Education and Socialization* edited by R. Corwin. Greenwood, CT: JAI Press, 131–59.

Borman, K. M. and Reisman, J., 1986. "Introduction" in *Becoming a Worker* edited by K. M. Borman and J. Reisman. Norwood, NJ: Ablex, 3–25.

Borus, M. and Carpenter, S., 1984. "Choices in Education" in *Youth and the Labor Market: Analysis of National Longitudinal Study* edited by M. Borus. W. E. Upjohn Institute of Employment Research.

Bourdieu, P. and Passeron, J., 1977. *Reproduction in Education, Society, and Culture.* Beverly Hills, CA: Sage.

Bowles, S. and Gintis, H., 1974. *Schooling in Capitalist America.* New York, NY: Basic.

Brake, M., 1980. *The Sociology of Youth Culture and Youth Subculture.* London, Routledge and Kegan Paul.

Braverman, H., 1974. *Labor and Monopoly Capital: The Degradation of Work in the Twentieth Century,* New York, NY: Monthly Press Review.

Bronfenbrenner, U., 1979. *The Ecology of Human Development: Experiments by Nature and Design.* Cambridge, MA: Harvard University Press.

Brown, C., 1982. "Dead End Jobs and Youth Unemployment" in *The Youth Labor Market* edited by R. Freeman and D. Wise. Chicago, IL: University of Chicago Press.

Burawoy, M. 1979. *Manufacturing Consent.* Chicago, IL: University of Chicago Press.

Burawoy, M., 1985. *The Politics of Production.* London: Verso.

Burbridge, L., 1985. "Dimensions of Youth Unemployment" in Proceedings of the Conference 1986: From School to Work: A School/Community Effort, Columbus, Ohio, Ohio Department of Education.

Carnoy, M. and Levin, H., 1985. *Schooling and Work in the Democratic State.* Stanford, CA: Stanford University Press.

Charner, I. and Fraser, B., 1987. *Youth and Work: What We Know; What We Don't Know; What We Need to Know.* Washington, DC: W. T. Grant Foundation Commission on Work, Family and Citizenship.

Charner, I. and Fraser, B., 1984. *Fast Food Jobs.* Washington, DC: National Institute for Work and Learning.

Cicourel, A. and Kitsuse, J., 1963. *The Educational Decision Makers.* Indianapolis, IN: Bobbs-Merrill.

Cincinnati Enquirer. September 27, 1987.

Clark, K. and Summers, L., 1979. "Demographic Differences in Cyclical Employment Variation." *Journal of Human Resources.* 16:1.

Clark, R. 1983. *Family Life and School Achievements: Why Poor Black Children Succeed or Fail.* Chicago, IL: University of Chicago Press.

Claus, J. F., 1986. *Opportunity or Inequality in Vocational Education?* Unpublished Ph.D. Dissertation.

Corwin, R. 1986. "Organizational Skills and the 'Deskilling' Hypothesis" in *Becoming a Worker* edited by K. Borman and J. Reisman. Norwood, NJ: Ablex.

Corwin, R. and Namboodiri K., 1989. "Have Individuals Been Over- Emphasized in School-Effects Research?" in *Review of Research in Education and Socialization* edited by K. Namboodiri and R. Corwin. Greenwood, CT: JAI Press, 141–176.

Csikszentmihaly, M. and Larson, P., 1984. *Being Adolescent.* New York, NY: Basic.

D'Amico, R. and Baker, P., 1985. "Early Labor Market Differentiation Among Terminal High School Graduates" in *Pathway to the Future.* Vol.5. Worthington, OH: Center for Human Resource Research.

DiMaggio, P., 1982. "Cultural Capital and School Success: The Impact of Status Culture Participation on the Grades of U.S. High School Students." *American Sociological Review.* 47:89–201.

Doeringer, P. and Piore, M., 1971. *Internal Labor Markets and Manpower Analysis.* Lexington, MA: Lexington Books.

Ekstrom, R. B., 1985. *Public High School Guidance Counseling; A Report to the College Board Commission on Precollege Guidance and Counseling.* Princeton, NJ: Educational Testing Service.

Ekstrom R. B., Goertz, M. E. and Rock, D. E., 1989. *Education and American Youth.* London: Falmer Press.

Epstein, C. F., 1990. "The Cultural Perspective and the Study of Work" in *The Nature of Work* edited by K. Erikson and S. P. Vallas. New Haven, CT: Yale University Press, 88–98.

Erickson, E., 1950. *Childhood and Society.* New York, NY: Norton.

Farley, R., 1984. *Blacks and Whites, Narrowing the Gap?* Cambridge, MA: Harvard University Press.

Fisher, B., 1967. *Industrial Education, Ideals and Institutions*, Madison, WI: University of Wisconsin Press.

Freeman, R. B. and Holzer, J. 1986. *The Black Youth Employment Crisis.* Chicago, IL: Chicago University Press.

Freeman, R. B. and Wise, D. A., 1982. *The Youth Labor Market Problem: It's Nature, Causes, and Consequences.* Chicago, IL: University of Chicago Press.

Gaskell, J., 1986. "Gender and Class in Clerical Training." Paper presented at the Conference on Women and Education, University of British Columbia, Vancouver, BC.

Gaskell, J. and Lazerson, M., 1980–81. "Between School and Work: Perspectives of Working Class Youth." *Interchange in Educational Policy.* 11:80–86.

Giroux, H., 1981. *Ideology, Culture and the Process of Schooling.* Philadelphia, PA: Temple University Press.

Giroux, H., 1983. *Theory and Resistance in Education: A Pedagogy for the Opposition.* Hadley, MA: Bergin and Garvey.

Gouldner, A. W., 1954. *Patterns of Industrial Bureaucracy.* Glencoe, IL: Free Press.

Grant, W. T. Commission on Work, Family and Citizenship, 1988. *The Forgotten Half: Non-College Youth in America.* Final Report, Youth and American's Future, The William T. Grant Foundation Commission on Work, Family and Citizenship, Washington, D.C.

Greenberger, E. and Steinberg, L., 1986. *When Teenagers Work.* New York, NY: Basic Books.

Greenberger, E., Steinberg, L., and Vaux, A., 1981. "Adolescents Who Work: Health and Behavioral Consequences of Job Stress." *Developmental Psychology.* 17:691–703.

Griffin, C., 1985. *Typical Girls?: Young Women from Schools to the Job Market.* London: Routledge and Kegan Paul.

Hahn, A. and Lerman, R., 1985. *What Works in Youth Employment Policy: How to Help Young Workers from Poor Families.* Washington, DC: National Planning Association.

Hall, R., 1986. *Dimensions of Work.* Beverly Hills, CA: Sage Publications.

Hammack, F., 1988. Reviewer's Comments to the Editor.

Herbst, P. G., 1974. *Socio-Technical Design.* London: Tavistock Publications.

Heyns, B., 1978. *Summer Learning and the Effects of Schooling.* New York, NY: Academic Press.

Hochschild, A., 1983. *The Managed Heart.* Berkeley, CA: University of California Press.

Holland, D. and Eisenhart, M., 1990. *Educated in Romance*. Chicago: University of Chicago Press.

Holtzberg, C. and Giovanni, M., 1981. "Anthropology and Industry: Reappraisal and New Drections" in *Annual Review of Anthropology* edited by B. Siegel, A. Beals, and A. Tyler. Palo Alto, California: Annual Reviews.

Kalleberg, A. and Loscocco, K., 1983. "Age Differences in Job Satisfaction." *American Sociological Review.* 48:78–90.

Kanter, R. M., 1977. *Work and Family in the United States: A Critical Review and Agenda for Research and Policy.* New York, NY: Russell Sage Foundation.

Kett, S., 1977. *Rites of Passage.* New York, NY: Basic Books.

Kimmel, M.S., 1987. "The Contemporary 'Crisis' of Masculinity in Historical Perspective" in *The Making of Masculinities* edited by H. Brod. Boston, MA: Allen and Unwin. 121–54.

Koch, E., 1982. "Quality of Working Life (QWL): Some Potential Applications to Education." *Urban Education*, Vol. 17, 2: 181–97.

Kohn, M. and Schooler, C., 1978. "The Reciprocal Effects of the Substantive Complexity of Work and Intellectual Flexibility: A Longitudinal Assessment. *American Journal of Sociology.* 84:24–52.

Kohn, M. and Schooler, C., 1982. "Job Conditions and Personality: A Longitudinal Assessment of their Reciprocal Effects." *American Journal of Sociology.* 87:1257–86.

Kohn, M. and Schooler, C., 1983. In collaboration with J. Miller, K. A. Miller, C. Schoenbech, and R. Schoenberg. *Work and Personality: An Inquiry into the Impact of Social Stratification.* Norwood, NJ: Ablex.

Lareau, A., 1989. *Home Advantage: Social Class and Parental Intervention in Elementary Education.* New York, NY: Falmer Press.

Levin, H. and Rumberger, R., 1983. "The Low-Skill Future of High Tech." *Technology Review.* 86: 18–21.

Lowe, G. S., 1987. *Women in the Administrative Revolution: The Feminizing of Clerical Work.* Toronto: University of Toronto Press.

Lundberg, C. C., 1969. "Person-focused Joking: Patterns and Function." *Human Organization:* 28: 22–28.

Lupton, T., 1976. "Shop Floor Behavior." In *Handbook of Work, Organization and Society* edited by R. Dubin. Chicago,IL: Rand McNally.

Macleod, J., 1987. *Ain't No Makin' It*. Boulder, CO: Westview.

Marsland, D., 1987. *Education and Youth*. London: Falmer Press.

McLaren, P., 1980. *Schooling as a Ritual Performance: Towards a Political Economy of Educational Symbols and Gestures*. London: Routledge and Kegan Paul.

Mellor, E., 1987. "Workers at the Minimum Wage or Less: Who They Are and the Jobs They Hold." *Monthly Labor Review.* 110:34–38.

Miller, G., 1981. *It's a Living*. New York, NY: St. Martins Press.

Morgan, B., 1975. "Autonomy and Negotiation in an Industrial Setting." *Sociology of Work and Occupations*, 2:203–27.

Mortimer, J., 1990. "Employment." In the *Encyclopedia of Adolescence* edited by R. Lerner, A. Peterson and J. Brooks-Gunn. New York, NY: Garland Press.

Mortimer, J. and Lorence, J., 1979. *Occupational Experience and the Self-Concept: A Longitudinal Study*. Paper presented at the annual meeting of the American Sociological Association.

Mortimer, J., Lorence, J. and Kunka, D., 1986. *Work, Family, and Personality: Transition to Adulthood*. Norwood, NJ: Ablex.

National Research Council. U.S. Committee on Women's Employment. 1986. In *Computer Chips and Paper Clips: Technology and Women's Employment* edited by H. Hartmann, R. Kraut, and L. Tilly. Washington, DC: National Academy Press.

Natriello, G., 1987. "The Changing Context for Research and Policy on the Transition Between High School and Entry Level Positions in the Workplace." Paper presented at the annual meeting of The American Educational Research Association, Washington, DC.

Noyelle, T. & Stanback, T., 1983. *Economic Transformation of American Cities*. Totowa, NJ: Reisman and Allenheld.

Oakes, J., 1985. *Keeping Track: How Schools Structure Inequality*. New Haven, CT: Yale University Press.

Ogbu, J., 1986. "Stockton, California, Revisited: Joining the Labor Force" in *Becoming A Worker* edited by K. Borman, and J. Reisman. Norwood, NJ: Ablex.

Osterman, P., 1980. *Getting Started: The Youth Labor Market*. Cambridge, MA: MIT Press.

Penn, E., 1986. "The Theater of Work: How Some Youths Get Better

Parts" in *Becoming a Worker* edited by K. Borman, and J. Reisman. Norwood, NJ: Ablex, 201–43.

Persell, C. and Cookson, P., 1987. "Microcomputers and Elite Boarding Schools: Educational Innovations and Social Reproduction." *Sociology of Education*. 60:123–34.

Rosenbaum, J., 1976. *Making Inequality*. New York, NY: Wiley.

Rosenbaum P. R., 1986. "Dropping Out of High School in the United States: An Observational Study." *Journal of Educational Statistics*. 11:207–24.

Roy, D. F., 1959–60. "Banana Time: Job Satisfaction and Informal Interaction." *Human Organization*. 18:158–68.

Sennett R. and Cobb J., 1972. *The Hidden Injuries of Class*. New York: NY: Vintage Books.

Simpson, I. H., 1989. "The Sociology of Work: Where Have the Workers Gone?" *Social Forces*. 67: 563–581.

Simon, R., 1983. "But Who Will Let Yo Do It? Counter-Hegemonic Possibilities for Work Education." *Journal of Education*. 165: 235–56.

Snedeker, B., 1981. *Hard Knocks: Preparing Youth for Work*. Baltimore, MD: Johns Hopkins University.

Spenner, K. I., 1983. "Deciphering Prometheus: Temporal Change in the Skill Level of Work." *American Sociological Review*, 48:824–37.

Stanback, T., 1981. *Services, The New Economy*. Montclair, NJ: Allanheld, Osmun.

Stanback, T. and Noyelle, T., 1982. *Cities in Transition*. Totowa, NJ: Allanheld, Osmun.

U.S. Department of Education, 1986. Current Statistics, Washington, DC.

Valli, L., 1986. *Becoming Clerical Workers*. Boston, MA: Routledge and Kegan Paul.

West, M. and Newton, P., 1983. *The Transition from School to Work*. London: Croom-Helm.

Willis, P., 1977. *Learning to Labour: How working Class Kids Get Working Class Jobs*. London: Saxon House.

Wirth, A. G., 1990. "The Violation of People at Work in Schools" in *Shaping the Superintendency* edited by William E. Eaton. New York, NY: Teachers College Press.

Wirth, A. G., 1989. "Towards a Post-Industrial Intelligence: Gadamer and Dewey as Guides." *Thresholds in Education.* 15: 6–9.

Wirth, A. G., 1984. "The Recycled Society: Technology, Education, and "Good Work". *Journal of Cooperative Education.* 20: 8–17.

Wirth, A. G., 1983. *Productive Work in Industry and School: Becoming a Person Again.* College Park, MD: University Press of America.

Zuboff, S., 1988. *In the Age of the Smart Machine: The Future of Work and Power.* New York, NY: Basic Books.

SUBJECT INDEX

A

Adolescence: *See also* Youth; and developmental issues, x, 22; 41–42, 55, 71; and gender differences, 18, 21; and occupational identity, 22, 25; social construction of, 25–26, 72–75, 77, 128; and work, 26, 71, 133

Administrative marketing specialist: at Midwest Insurance, 96, 104; and patterns of authority, 99–104; task technology, 98–99; and training, 97, 98–99

African-Americans: and discrimination, 96, 125; in high school, 8–20; in labor force, 33, 36; and minimum wage, 35; and youth jobs, 4, 22, 41–47, 134–135

Age cohorts: x, 1, 36, 40

Alcohol Use: *See also* Drug Use; in high school, 66; and driving, 66; and leisure, 72; and work, 66

American Banking Institute (ABI): 95

American Youth Commission (1942): ix

Appliance repair worker: 39–40, 130

Apprenticeship: 108–109

Athletics: *See* Sports

Authority: in Clifton Coin and Stamp, 114–118; in fastener factory, 60–63; in Midland Bank, 85–90; in Midwest Insurance, 99–104; patterns of, 34, 36, 56, 58, 83; in River City Bank, 96; in sheet metal shop, 69–75; in Swedish Fitness, 120–126

B

Banks: 38, 42–47; and employee monitoring, 80, 85–87, 136; hiring, 79; as large and bureaucratized, 82–83, 90,104; technological change, 79–83

Blacks: *See also* African-Americans

Bookkeeping clerk: *See also* Clerical Jobs; and job task technology, 94–96; and patterns of authority, 96; at River City Bank, 93–96, 100

Bureau of Labor Statistics: 33, (table), 105–106

AUTHOR INDEX

DUE DATE

	MAY 0 1 1993		
	JUN 13 1994		
	APR 0 8 199		
			Printed in USA